About Ray Hawkins

Ray was born just before Christmas in 1938 at Rockdale, New South Wales to working class parents. After achieving the Intermediate School Certificate he worked as a lathe operator for a car engine repair firm then a labourer with his father's light steel fabrication business. He was sent to Sunday school at the local Church of Christ where he made his confession of faith and was baptized. At 21 years he was accepted as a student at the Churches of Christ Woolwich Bible College (Sydney). In 1963 Ray became the Student President of the College. That year he met his wife-to-be, Mary, who came to College for a two year missionary course. In 1964 they were married and over the years they became parents of three children.

Their major ministry emphasis has been in establishing two new Churches in NSW and preventing one from closure in Queensland. They also ministered in England. Ray has been NSW Conference President on two occasions, and NSW President for the Ministers' Association. He has been a Chaplain at the Green Hills Retirement village and Nursing Home (NSW). For 18 years he was involved with the Tenambit/Morpeth Rotary club becoming President and later made a 'Paul Harris Fellow'. Ray also became active with the 'Walk to Emmaus' movement and was Community Spiritual Director for Tasmania.

In his later years he went with Mary three times as part of short term mission trips to Africa. Out of that experience he wrote the 31 day devotional 'The Neurotic Rooster.' (It was a finance raiser for Eagles Wings in Zambia.) Now retired to Beauty Point, Tasmania, with Mary (who is a multi-published Inspirational Romance writer) he still preaches and is involved in establishing a Christian Fellowship there.

He is a regular contributor to 'The Upper Room' devotional magazine as well as having numerous articles, poems and studies from Scripture printed throughout his ministry. More information about Ray on www.mary-hawkins.com.

Bethlehem's Warrior Baby
Published by Even Before Publishing;
a division of Wombat Books
P. O. Box 1519, Capalaba Qld 4157
www.evenbeforepublishing.com
www.wombatbooks.com.au

© Ray Hawkins 2012
Design and layout by Even Before Publishing

National Library of Australia Cataloguing-in-Publication entry
Author: Hawkins, Raymond.
Title: Bethlehem's warrior baby : 31 biblical devotions to meditate on the Christmas conquest / Hawkins, Ray.
ISBN: 9781922074461 (pbk.)
Subjects: Jesus Christ--Devotional literature.
            Christmas.
Dewey Number: 232.92

All rights reserved. No part of this publication may be reproduced, stored in, or introduced into a retrieval system, or transmitted, in any form, or by any means (electronic, mechanical, photocopying, recording or otherwise) without the prior written permission of the publisher.

Unless otherwise indicated all Bible quotes are from the New International Version.

Bethlehem's Warrior Baby

31 Biblical Devotions to Meditate on the Christmas Conquest

Dedication
To our children and grandchildren
God's extra gifts to Ray and Mary.

Contents

About Ray Hawkins

Introduction

Someone Is Coming
Day: 1   *12*

The Promised One Foreshadowed
Day: 2   *14*

The Prophet Like Unto Moses
Day: 3   *17*

The Christmas Sign
Day: 4   *19*

Light In The Midst Of Darkness
Day : 5   *21*

The Warrior Baby
Day: 6   *23*

The Disturbing Angel
Day:7   *25*

Why The Family 'Tree' of Jesus?
Day: 8   *27*

Did The Angels Get It Wrong?
Day: 9   *29*

The Magnificat – A Warrior's Song
Day: 10   *31*

The Herald of Christmas
Day:11   *33*

Christmas Expresses God's Heart
Day: 12   *35*

Behold Your Salvation
Day: 13   *37*

A Body Prepared
Day: 14   *39*

The Time Has Arrived
Day: 15   *41*

Christmas – When God Arrived
Day: 16   *43*

Christmas in Contrast
Day: 17   *45*

Emmanuel
Day: 18   *47*

From What Does Christ Save Us?
Day: 19   *49*

'The Light of Life'
Day: 20   *51*

Choices Jesus Made
Day: 21   *53*

Heavenly Bread
Day: 22   *55*

No Reputation
Day: 23   *57*

Jacob's Promise to Judah
Day: 24   *59*

Wonderful Counsellor
Day: 25   *61*

Mighty God	
Day: 26	*63*
Everlasting Father	
Day: 27	*66*
Prince of Peace	
Day: 28	*68*
Mystery Men	
Day: 29	*70*
He's a Star!	
Day: 30	*72*
Giving is the Joy of Christmas	
Day: 31	*74*
The Battle Cry of Christmas	

Introduction

Reading: John 1:1-18

Christmas is a declaration of war!

We have made it what it was never intended to be, a sweet, sentimental occasion for people to have nice, warm, fuzzy feelings.

The idea that someone is coming permeates the first thirty-nine books of the Bible. In many places there are clues to His identity and purpose, bold statements about His character and strategy. There are also metaphors pointing to the spiritual realities the coming One would fulfil.

The god of this world is no fool. As you study the Old Testament you are given insights into his attempts to prevent the Promised One from coming. This included attempts to destroy the nation of Israel, corrupt and obliterate the genealogical line and mutilate the message. Time after time it seemed Satan came close to achieving his aims. The Lord God of Hosts always came up with an answer, a master stroke, a surprise element.

Herod produced the first martyrs of Christmas. On hearing about the birth of the Promised One he ordered the death of babes two years and under in Bethlehem. That this 'Someone' had finally come was declared by the shepherds, the Magi and others. The four Gospels present their majestic portrayals of the One called Jesus. It becomes clear from their writings they were convinced that this man of Nazareth was the fulfilment of the clues, metaphors and other snippets from their Scriptures. Jesus himself insisted that people examine Him and the Scriptures to make sure they matched (John 5:39).

Jesus had a strategy for re-conquering the world and saving it from the powers of Darkness. Such a plan included enlisting men and women to His cause. They had to be convinced about Him and what He was on about. The Lord never bribed people to join his ranks. In fact, Jesus spelled out loud and clear the costs involved in following Him.

The following thirty-one devotional meditations take you into an understanding of the 'Battle Zone'. You will follow God's promise of the One who is to come and how each 'jigsaw' piece would ultimately come together at Bethlehem. Being convinced about who Jesus is, why he came, and the victory achieved gives us moral and spiritual courage. We need this to face the challenges of being in the legion of the Lord.

Throughout both Testaments is a third facet of the coming of the Promised One. It is the statement: 'Someone' is coming *again*! It is the same Jesus who came the first time to experience the cross, rise again and offer us salvation and a new destiny. When He comes again it will be to judge the world and to reign in righteousness. Those who by faith have declared their allegiance will in that day share in His kingdom.

Though the contest continues, victory is assured. Be strengthened for the conflict through insights from these devotional meditations!

Raymond N. Hawkins

Someone Is Coming

Day: 1

Reading: Genesis 3:1-15

There is so much that is missing from the Biblical account. This is understandable. The collection of accounts in the sixty-six books would be far larger if everything was included, but these passages wouldn't necessarily add anything that the Lord considered important. We just have to accept what Deuteronomy 29:29 says on this matter, 'The secret things belong to the Lord our God, but the things revealed belong to us and to our children forever, that we may follow all the words of this law.' Still, I often wonder about some of those unrecorded events. For example: In the opening chapters of Genesis, how long did Adam and Eve spend in the Garden? When did the rebellion by Lucifer, the shining one, take place? In a sense, knowing wouldn't change the facts, just settle my curiosity.

This we know: when the Godhead decided to create Adam and Eve, Christmas and Easter became a necessity (Genesis 1:27, 28). God is never taken by surprise, so He knew Adam would betray His trust and hand over the 'deeds' of earth's dominion to the Deceiver. The Lord God was also aware that such a betrayal would birth Death and Sin (Romans 5:12-14). It would also give the descendants of Adam and Eve a 'god is me' complex. Each and every facet of Adam's treason had to be dealt with and that would require a Second Adam. He had to be one who was perfect, yet who was also flesh and blood with a family history. All this and more is bound up in the statement of intent made by the Eternal God to Satan in Genesis 3:15.

The word 'seed' is a more specialised expression for what was to take place than offspring. The seed of the woman points to someone special. The apostle Paul clarifies the difference between 'seed' and 'offspring' in Galatians 3:16: 'The promises were spoken to Abraham and to his seed. Scripture does not say "and to seeds", meaning many people, but "and to your seed", meaning one person, who is Christ.' It doesn't put a time scale to it, nor highlight a specific place. It is a simple statement, a throwing down the gauntlet to the usurper. God does not give up His sovereign rule over any part of His creation. Throughout the Old Testament there is the sense of 'Someone' coming. It is this atmosphere which an honest reader of the first thirty-nine books breathes in as he or she follows the account of God's dealings with individuals, families and nations.

To understand and appreciate Christmas requires us to view it as the beginning of a life and death contest. Christmas is the culmination of centuries of planning by God, not for His sake, but for ours. He wanted us to know that the 'Someone' promised had come. He would be recognised by comparing all the clues and seeing them fulfilled in that person and no one else. Each clue would be similar to a jigsaw piece. By itself it would tantalise without revealing much. When interlocked with another piece a picture would begin to emerge. As we consider the various scriptural jigsaw pieces through these devotional readings we come face-to-face with the call of combat. The Lord God issued this when He said, 'I will put enmity between you (the Serpent) and the woman, and between your offspring (seed) and hers; he will crush your head and you will strike his heel.' (Genesis 3:15). We will also realise the significance of what Jesus said in John 5:39 'You diligently study the Scriptures ... These are the Scriptures which speak of me.'

Christmas is Heaven's invasion strategy to reclaim that which was stolen by deception. The powers of Darkness knew what was coming and tried to thwart it, corrupt it and destroy it even in the planning stages.

Prayer: I thank you, Eternal Lord, that you did not leave us, the descendents of Adam and Eve, in the power of Darkness and the fear of Death. Thank you for the meaning of Christmas. I have also experienced it in my own life, for which I praise your Name.

My gift to you today is to worship you in spirit and in truth in my everyday affairs.

The Promised One Foreshadowed

Day: 2

Reading: Genesis 12:1-8

God can be so unsettling. Just ask Abram. He wasn't a young man when God said to him 'leave' and begin a pilgrimage. To make this more difficult, the destination wasn't mentioned. He would know it when God said, 'This is it!' We're not told how God and Abram got together, all we know is Abram agreed and went. That was the beginning of his faith.

This descendent of Shem must have been intrigued by Yahweh's unconditional promise. What was wrapped up in the word 'blessing'? No details are given. In Genesis 12:7 the land issue is settled when they arrived in Canaan. The Lord said it would belong to Abram's offspring. Due to the silence in the New Testament, we are not permitted to limit this to the Messiah. In the context of Genesis 12 the promise is to Abraham's descendents. The Promised One was now gaining a family history and a national identity in the making.

From our perspective, and without any disrespect, God can seem so irritating to us. The promise is given. A male child is projected. Then silence. Time passes. No seed. How did Abram feel? What about Sarah? Then in Genesis 12, God breaks into this mundane scene with renewed encouragement which must have seemed like 'salt in a wound'. There would be a multitude of his descendents and they would possess the land. But where was the child who would make it possible?

Abram's tenacious faith is astounding, even allowing for some high profile mistakes. Then when he is ninety-nine Yahweh appears to him and begins to bring the promise together. From Abram (exalted father) he is called Abraham (father of many). The impossible will become possible due to Yahweh's overruling. Isaac is born. It's a miracle birth. Sarah was the barren one until the Holy Spirit healed her. As with anything God does, there was a message wrapped up in this real life drama. It pointed down the centuries to Christmas. Then the miracle birth of the Messiah, previously foreshadowed in the birth of Isaac, would be fulfilled.

For the Promised One to come into this world on a multi-faceted mission, He would need a genealogy to verify His humanity. This requires a family and therefore a national identity. This being so, such factors must have the 'fingerprint' of God on them. Abraham's other children through Hagar (Genesis 16) and Keturah (Genesis 25:1) did not have this 'fingerprint'. It is through the son of promise the Promised One must come. Isaac had two sons, Jacob and Esau, and both became nations. It is through Jacob that we can trace the 'fingerprint' of God. This virile man was father to twelve sons and at least one daughter we know about. How can we be sure from which line the Messiah would come? Again, this goes beyond the expected procedures relating to the privileges of the first born. Judah, the fourth born, is chosen by a prophetic announcement by Jacob. The son's name means 'praise', and how appropriate this name would be over the person and work of the Promised One. Judah is the kingly line and the Messiah would bear that title over the nation.

'Judah, your brothers will praise you; your hand will be on the neck of your enemies; your father's sons will bow down to you. You are a lion's cub, O Judah; you return from the prey my son ... The sceptre will not depart from Judah, nor the ruler's staff from between his feet, until he comes to whom it belongs and the obedience of the nations is his.' (Jacob's prophecy in Genesis 49:8-10).

The thirty-nine books of the Old Testament continually highlight the 'fingerprints' of God. These allow us to trace His purposes. That's why the genealogies, recorded in Matthew and Luke, are so important for the Church and the nation of Israel today. Once again, we see the unrestricted scope of God's grace and glory even in an apparent minor detail, such as preserving Christ Jesus' human forebears. Without this we could not check out His lineage, as the Roman legions destroyed the Jewish temple and archives in AD70. I find it fascinating that a book for Christians preserves the lineage of Israel's King, Jesus.

Mary sums it up beautifully as she concludes what is called her 'Magnificat'. '(God) has helped His servant Israel, remembering to be merciful to Abraham and his descendents for ever, even as He said to our fathers.' (Luke 1:54-55).

The blessing promised through Abraham, Isaac and Jacob is Jesus, the Messiah, King of Israel, Lord of all.

Prayer: Eternal God, I stand in awe before you as I appreciate anew, and in a deeper way, how you fulfil your promises in the face of great difficulties and human weaknesses. Thank you for the testimony of Christmas and the blessing you want us to enjoy in the Lord Jesus.

My gift: I have nothing to offer you that would express my gratitude. I can only wrap myself up in your grace to be a living sacrifice that honours you.

The Prophet Like Unto Moses
Day: 3

Readings: Deuteronomy 18:15-22, John 1:19-25

When a child is born, relatives gather around to discuss or discover family likenesses. There is that genetic miracle of DNA that affects hereditary. In the Scriptures there is also a spiritual DNA that must be found in the Promised One. One of those 'chromosomes' must point to Moses.

The Lord God was going to 'raise up' this special envoy of Heaven. The Devil is the master counterfeiter, so God has built into the 'gene pool' unmistakeable pointers to the genuine Promised One. Peter informed us in 1 Peter 1:10-12 how the ancients studied the writings to recognise Him when He came. We know from the passage that even the angels seemed occupied with this.

When John the Baptiser came on the scene, the religious authorities wanted to know if he had the genes of 'the promised Prophet'. He told them no, but that person was coming. Indeed, He was on the scene already.

There are many similarities between Moses and Jesus. Let us consider just some of them. In both cases Israel was under foreign domination. When Moses was born he was under threat of infanticide due to Pharaoh's paranoia. Jesus as a babe, likewise, was under a death threat from Herod's madness. Later on, Moses was Yahweh's mediator of the Mount Sinai religious, moral and relational Law. When Jesus dared to say in Matthew 5:21, 'you have heard it said … but I tell unto you' He was claiming higher status than Moses. How? Because Jesus came to fulfil the Law of Moses! (Matt 5:17). Heaven testified to this at His baptism and on the mount of Transfiguration.

Throughout His ministry people wrestled with the dilemma of a miracle working rabbi from Nazareth and the promised Prophet. The woman at the well saw him as a prophet. The people at the Feast of Tabernacles debated his credentials, saying 'Surely, this is the prophet.' When Jesus rode in to Jerusalem the crowd hailed Him as 'This is Jesus, the prophet from Nazareth in Galilee.' Such comments had little effect on the people. Only after the resurrection would the significance of what they said dawn upon them. The same is true today when we only see Jesus as teacher or healer and fail to grasp Him as the risen Lord of glory.

In Numbers 12:6-8 there is a revealing statement: 'When a prophet of the Lord is among you, I reveal myself to him in visions, I speak to him in dreams. But this is not true of my servant Moses; he is faithful in all my house. With him I speak face to face, clearly and not in riddles; he sees the form of the Lord.'

This is the first instance where Moses is given the Bible's high title of 'servant'. He is also called that in Deuteronomy and Joshua. A term many find offensive and demeaning is held in high esteem by Heaven. Isaiah is the prophet who unveils the role of God's Promised One as Servant. Such passages as chapters 42, 49, 50 and 53 of Isaiah are references which point to Jesus.

A recurring feature in John's Gospel is Jesus having face-to-face intimacy with His heavenly Father. John 5:19, 20: 'I tell you the truth, the Son can do nothing by himself; he can do only what he sees his Father doing ... the Father loves the Son and shows him all he does.' Verse 30 adds, 'By myself I can do nothing; I judge only as I hear, and my judgement is just, for I seek not to please myself but him who sent me.' (Compare with 5:36-47). Here is the fulfilment of 'I will put my words in his mouth'.

It is on this foundation that a man or woman must take seriously what Jesus said and shared with His disciples. Failure to do this will result in the other matter of being a prophet like unto Moses. His words will bring judgement.

As you celebrate Christmas, consider again the scriptural insights into the spiritual DNA of Jesus. He is the Promised Prophet.

Prayer: Lord Jesus, lead me into a deeper appreciation of yourself. Help me understand what it means to call you 'The Prophet promised in the mould of Moses'. May I hear and heed your word as I praise you, my Lawgiver and Deliverer.

My gift: Receive I pray this gift of a humble, obedient heart wherein your word may dwell.

The Christmas Sign

Day: 4

Reading: Isaiah 7:10-16, Luke 2:8-12

Moses captured the enslaved Israelites' attention through the signs and wonders Yahweh did through him. Until then, it would seem that the people were in a dejected and defeated mood. The Lord God also revealed the impotency of Egypt's idols at the same time. The ten plagues were God's declaration that He, and He alone, is sovereign. As such, He will bring judgement upon the gods of the nations (Exodus 12:12).

Signs became a feature of the Eternal God's dealings with the people of Israel. The apostle Paul expresses this in 1 Corinthians 1:22: 'Jews demand miraculous signs and Greeks look for wisdom.' Time and again in His ministry Jesus was asked for a sign, presumably from Heaven, that would verify who He was and what He did. Why they couldn't grasp His miracles as such is beyond understanding. Jesus, however, did give them one sign, the sign of Jonah (Matthew 12:38,39).

There is another sign, God given, which validates Christmas for all – especially a Jewish person. It was given at the Lord's direction through Isaiah to King Ahaz that a virgin would bring forth a child and call his name Emmanuel (Isaiah 7:14). The sign would be from Yahweh and done by Him. Somehow or other, God would bring this sign to fruition without the power, cunning or strategy of man.

It was that glorious night the angels shattered the Bethlehem darkness when the promised sign came into being. Luke 2:11-12: 'Today in the town of David a Saviour has been born to you; he is Christ the Lord. This will be a sign to you: you will find a baby wrapped in cloths and lying in a manager.' What was so striking about this birth? We know the story so well that we miss the emotional aspects of it. How would anyone have known the details of Jesus' birth unless Mary and Joseph, at God's direction, told Matthew and Luke! The intimacy of pregnancy and, in Mary and Joseph's case, the potential for embarrassment and misunderstanding, reveals how important the uncovering of this sign was. It remains so today!

You can imagine the innuendoes, wagging tongues and slander that erupted when the Gospel began circulating. Who would put themselves into such an emotional and religious cauldron if the birth of Jesus had not taken place this way? Then again, if He had never risen from the dead, no one would have been interested. Therefore, what is recorded about the birth of Jesus is to authenticate it as the fulfilment of the Isaiah declaration. Matthew makes this quite clear when he writes what the angel of the Lord said to Joseph: 'Joseph son of David, do not be afraid to take Mary home as your wife, because what is conceived in her is from the Holy Spirit. She will give birth to a son, because he will save his people from their sins all this took place to fulfil what the Lord had said through the prophet: The virgin will be with child and will give birth to a son, and they will call him Immanuel – which means, 'God with us.' (Matthew 1:20-23).

Some think it unimportant to stress the virgin birth of Jesus. Part of their claim comes from the paucity of direct reference to it in the Epistles. However, the necessity for such a birth is everywhere inferred. Without it Jesus could not have been the second Adam; Jesus could not have been sinless, for He would have had a soul nature corrupted by the fall; His human spirit would have been dead to God (Ephesians 2:1-4); if He was born of 'the flesh' then He would be blemished in the sight of God the Father. There is no way Jesus' crucifixion would be able to deal with humankind's sin through substitution and identification, for He would have been in need of saving Himself.

Prayer: Heavenly Father, thank you for the willingness of Mary and Joseph to be partners in your Christmas sign. Thank you for their acceptance of the pain and shame it would arouse in some. We honour them and ask that we, too, might be prepared to wear any shame others might throw on us because we serve Jesus as the Christ.

My gift: I may not be a 'sign' but I'm willing to be a signpost pointing to you in my everyday life.

Light In The Midst Of Darkness
Day : 5

Reading: Isaiah 8:19-9:7, Matthew 4:12-16

On our honeymoon, my wife and I went down a tourist cave. The cavern was beautifully lit and welcoming. Then they turned off the lights. Complete darkness. The result was oppressive, suffocating and, for a person like my wife Mary who suffers with claustrophobia, quite frightening. To be left without light can mean a panic attack (which she suffered), despair and, ultimately, even death. The relief when the lights were switched on was overwhelming.

Isaiah's picture of a nation in darkness has that same sense of foreboding. The Darkness which had enveloped the people was moral and spiritual. Also implied is a military suppression of the nation's liberty through defeat and loss of sovereignty. Instead of crying out to Yahweh, the people consulted mediums and spiritists, deepening their darkness further. 'Then they will look toward the earth and see only distress and darkness and fearful gloom, and they will be thrust into utter darkness.' (Isaiah 8:22).

If Isaiah had finished his word at that point what a horrible picture it would have been. 'Nevertheless ... the people walking in great darkness have seen a great light; on those living in the land of the shadow of death a light has dawned.' (Isaiah 9:1,2). That 'nevertheless' offers hope.

The startling thing in this passage is Isaiah's verdict on what 'the light' would be. In Isaiah 9:6-7 he defines it as 'a child' and 'a son'. Once again, the Biblical stress upon a Promised One, a babe born of a virgin, rises to the forefront. I wonder how the hearers of Isaiah's prophecy felt as they weighed up the apparent strength of the Darkness against that of a baby in swaddling cloths. This baby boy, however, was something special, someone the Darkness would fear. This is grasped in the titles He wore. Each one has eternal significance. Consider them: Wonderful Counsellor, Mighty God, Everlasting Father, Prince of Peace. More than that, He is the head of an everlasting government in fulfilment of God's covenant with David.

The very idea of this happening must have sent shock waves rumbling through the Kingdom of Darkness. This could not be allowed to happen.

When you read the history of Israel in the light of Isaiah's prophecy, you sense a concerted effort by the Darkness to corrupt and crush the Davidic line. The Babylonian captivity and destitute state of the descendents of David afterwards gave the Darkness the apparent advantage.

When Jesus comes onto the scene as a babe, the apostle John called Him The Word. Just as significantly, John also wrote, 'In him was life, and that life was the light of men. The light shines in the darkness, but the darkness has not understood it.' (John 1:4, 5). In the footnotes the NIV says the word 'understood' could also mean 'overcomes'. The Darkness tried. It failed!

Christmas continues to draw our attention to the struggle between light and darkness, life and death. Many who enjoy 'Christmas' only want the holiday, the partying and the presents. Such attitudes are not in themselves wrong. Without the knowledge of Jesus as the source and meaning of Christmas, however, all that happens is a vain attempt to make the Darkness endurable.

Matthew draws our attention to the importance of the appearance of Jesus onto the spiritual and political scene of Israel. In chapter 4:13-16 he quotes Isaiah 9:1,2. Where did all this begin? Not in Bethlehem, the place of birth, but where Jesus grew up as a child – Galilee of the Gentiles! What was the situation of His era? Military oppression by Rome, moral and religious confusion; the people under the burden of darkness! Into this Jesus walked. The sadness He encountered is written in John 3:19: 'This is the verdict: Light has come into the world, but men loved darkness instead of light because their deeds were evil.'

At Christmas time there are many reasons to celebrate. One is the constant reminder that God did not leave the world in a state of devilish darkness. John 8:12: 'When Jesus spoke to the people, He said, I am the light of the world. Whoever follows me will never walk in darkness, but will have the light of life.' The promised child of Isaiah 9 is none other than the Babe of Bethlehem, the resident of Galilee of the Gentiles. He is the Light of the World.

Prayer: For taking those who put their trust in you, wonderful Lord, we give you our eternal gratitude that you take them out of the Kingdom of Darkness. We thank you also that your Word is a lamp to our feet and a light to our path as we make our journey home.

My Gift: I desire that you find pleasure in making me a light bearer to light up the way for others to see you as the Light of their world.

The Warrior Baby

Day: 6

Reading: Micah 4:9-5:5a

Some children, it is said, are born 'with a silver spoon in their mouth'. Others are not so fortunate. When Jesus was born, what would you 'see' in His mouth? Some like to think it would be an 'olive leaf'. Micah the prophet saw a sword. His picture of what we call Christmas is cloaked in military terms. This may be coloured by the times in which he lived as well as the future he perceived. Jesus endorsed this idea. Matthew 10:34: 'Do not suppose that I have come to bring peace to the earth. I did not come to bring peace, but a sword.'

In the midst of troublesome times a Babe would be born who is God's appointed ruler. At the mention of Bethlehem, Ephrathah points back as well as forward. The backward glance is to King David, the warrior ruler who was also the founder of the 'Shepherd kings' of Judah. The forward look pierces the centuries and brings us to the birth of Jesus in that town. He is the descendent of David on both sides of the family 'tree'.

Over the preceding centuries Bethlehem was a military base, first for the Philistines, then Rehoboam, and, at Jesus' birth, by Herod. The mighty Herodian fort was on the outskirts of the town and cast its shadow over it. Once again, Scripture throws into stark contrast the forces of the world and the apparent weakness of God's plans.

This child's 'origins', or as otherwise translated, 'goings out', are 'from old, from ancient times'. What do you think Micah is trying to express? His pushes us back beyond the commencement of the Davidic dynasty. The emphasis on 'of old, from ancient times' brings us into touch with eternity. The word 'ancient times' is translated in the King James version as 'everlasting'. It can be cross referenced to Psalm 90:2: 'Before the mountains were born or you brought forth the earth and the world, from everlasting to everlasting you are God.' Surely, this is the mind stretching and faith demanding dimension of a Biblical concept of Jesus.

The prophet, living prior to the Babylonian captivity, foretold Israel's abandonment by God. This was not a casting away. It was a judgement foretold on disobedience. In the words of Amos (8:11) it would include a famine. 'The days are coming declares the Sovereign Lord, when I will send a famine through the land – not a famine of food or a thirst for water, but a famine of hearing the words of the Lord.' This abandonment, this famine, would end when a woman goes into child labour and brings forth the Promised One. Christmas is the drought breaker. God shatters Heaven's silence. He has spoken through His only begotten. No longer is He far away. He is Emmanuel, God with us.

Micah didn't know the Child's Name. We do! Micah did know what this Promised One would do. 'He will stand and shepherd His flock in the strength of the Lord in the majesty of the Lord His God ... and He will be their peace.' For reasons beyond what this devotional can cover, it has not yet happened. As surely as the longed for coming of the promised child was fulfilled, so will the rest of what Micah has said come to pass.

What was the 'sword in the cradle'?

It was the sword of the Spirit, the Word of God, which He would wield against the forces of darkness, the Devil and the evil intent of the human heart. It was the sword for fulfilling Heaven's plan of salvation and restoration. It was the sword of the Son of God, who would wage war by laying down His life on the cross in apparent defeat. When He rose triumphant from the tomb, He held that sword intact. It is this sword which He has placed into the hands of His disciples. Hebrews 4:12: 'The word of God is living and active. Sharper than any double-edged sword, it penetrates even to dividing soul and spirit, joints and marrow; it judges the thoughts and attitudes of the heart.' This is why we are told to 'preach the word, in season and out of season.'

According to Revelation 19, there is another sword the Lord Jesus will one day grasp. That sword of conquest is for another 'day'.

Prayer: To kneel before you as your servant is an honour beyond any comparison. I praise you, my Sovereign Lord, for wielding your sword in my heart and mind, revealing and destroying its darkness and self enthronement.

My gift: My mouth to speak your truth; my heart your castle; my hands to serve others in your Name; my feet to walk in your steps.

The Disturbing Angel

Day:7

Reading: Luke 1:26-38

What an errand for an angel.

It was so important the archangel Gabriel was commissioned. Gabriel's name means 'God is mighty' and yet he was given the task of announcing a baby's conception. It seems, on the surface, a small time matter for such a heavenly being! Was it? Not when this baby was the longed for Promised One.

We are not told when or exactly where it was that Gabriel stepped into Mary's world. We only know it was in Nazareth. Her apprehension must have been evident, for his opening words were 'be of good cheer, rejoice!' Luke records she was greatly troubled and I wonder if that statement from the angel quieted her thumping heart. Throughout Scripture, the appearance of an angel had similar affects on people. Mary was no different.

Gabriel reassured her with 'Do not be afraid, you have found favour with God.' That, at least, would have given her time to catch her breath. Was there any pause by Gabriel, or was he too excited with the message he had to give? What he went on to say must have aroused many and varied emotions in this wonderful young woman. Here she was, honoured to be the chosen one to carry the promised baby. The longing of all devout Jewish maidens was to be hers, but she wasn't married – betrothed yes, but not married. In a small town such as Nazareth there would be no place to hide her pregnancy. What would Joseph say? Would he believe her story? (No wonder an angel had to confirm the story to him!) The event we call Christmas was surrounded with a myriad of emotional and logistical difficulties. The walk of the faithful isn't always smooth. It can also be costly emotionally and relationally. People persevere with it because of God's calling and grace.

Mary and Joseph could not even choose the Child's name. This was Heaven's prerogative. As most readers of the Old Testament know, names have important significance in God's purposes. The ones chosen for this baby would reveal His person and His mission. Jesus in Hebrew is 'Joshua' which means, 'Yahweh saves'. The name Immanuel means 'God with us'. Mary's role was to provide the human heritage that would clothe the unique and only begotten Son of God. The verification of both aspects of the Promised One, now revealed, is found in Romans 1:2-4. '... the Gospel he promised beforehand through his prophets in the Holy Scriptures regarding his Son, who as to his human nature was a descendent of David and who through the Spirit of holiness was declared with power to be the Son of God, by his resurrection from the dead: Jesus Christ our Lord.'

This Jesus is heir to the Davidic throne. Where is that situated? In Jerusalem! Should it be taken literally in today's political climate or should the gentile Church spiritualise it? Gabriel had no doubts. The prophets Isaiah and Zechariah, and others, had no doubt. It is a literal promise with a literal, future fulfilment. The prophets are unanimous in mentioning the fact that the right to ascend the throne will not be given to Him by the World powers. Significant then, becomes the choice of the Hebrew name, Joshua. This man was a leader and warrior of Israel. His namesake is in the same mould. His mission is to fulfil the word of God in all its majesty and mystery.

Do you wonder, as I do, what Mary thought of this? It seemed so preposterous when her people were slaves in their own country, courtesy of the might of the Roman legions. From Luke 1:46-55 we read it didn't shock her.

However, the message of Gabriel is still disturbing men and women. It confronts them with an historic person with an unbelievable mission. The records spanning over four thousand years up to His birth are His credentials. To believe Jesus is the Promised One drives us to consider what took Him to the cross. Then we cannot hide from the wonder of His resurrection victory. We are faced with a choice – hope it isn't true so we can live as we please, or to make Mary's words our own, 'I am the Lord's servant'.

Prayer: On the truth of your word, Almighty God, I am drawn to you through Jesus the Lord and Saviour. You have disturbed me to the point where I know I will only find peace and wholeness in yielding my life to you. Thank you for accepting me.

My gift to you is myself. Some would consider it a flawed gift; rightly so, but it is all I have to offer.

Why The Family 'Tree' of Jesus?
Day: 8
Reading: Matthew 1:1-17, Luke 3:23-37

Mary and I have enjoyed doing research into our family tree. It's fascinating to realise our hereditary and our personality come from others, courtesy of the miracle of DNA. We still make our choices which will influence our children and their children, and yet our present is coloured by our unknown past.

In the Jewish world the family 'tree' was vitally important in regards to kingship and their religious system. The Davidic and the Levitical 'branches' were mandatory for authentic claims to rule and to serve at the temple. The latter is written about in the books of Ezra and Nehemiah. Why? Because some returnees from Babylon made claims to the priesthood, but could not furnish proof of their forebears. They were, therefore, excluded.

If Jesus is to have any credibility in His claim to be a descendent of the Royal household, it must be on record. Before the destruction of the temple and its archives such a claim could easily be examined. After AD70 this became impossible. The two accounts in the Gospels of Matthew and Luke are therefore of vital importance. These would have been researched by the writers long before the temple's destruction, and people of the day would have soon revealed any discrepancies. How wonderful that what is considered Christian literature is actually the 'vault' for the safe keeping of Jesus' hereditary right to the throne of Israel.

If we are to take the Scriptures seriously, then we will understand the implications behind the constant references to the Promised One as the ruler in Jerusalem on the throne of David forever! Some may be concerned at the apparent differences in the two accounts. One line comes from David through Solomon, the other from David via Nathan. Why? Joseph's line goes back to Solomon. This becomes a problem because of what Jeremiah prophesied in chapter 36:30, '... this is what the Lord says about Jehoiakim king of Judah, He will have no one to sit on the throne of David ...' In Jeremiah 22:30 this judgement from God is re-enforced in Jehoiakim's son, Jehoiachin; 'Record this man as if childless ... for none of his offspring will prosper, none will sit on the throne of David or rule any more in Judah.' If Jesus is of that 'branch', He is debarred from the throne.

The significance of Luke's account cannot be exaggerated. It unfolds Mary's genealogy which the writer takes back to Adam. In chapter 3:23 Luke uses an important few words, 'He (Jesus) was the son, so it was thought, of Joseph.' Once again we are thrown back upon the necessity of the virgin birth. No descendent of Solomon can legitimately occupy the throne. Jesus' human DNA comes from Nathan, born of David and Bathsheba.

According to scripture, there is also another aspect to the need for the virgin birth. It's expressed in Hebrew's 10:5-7: '... when Christ came into the world, He said: "Sacrifice and offering you did not desire, but a body you prepared for me; with burnt offerings and sin offerings you were not pleased." Then I said, "Here I am – it is written about me in the scroll – I have come to do your will, O God.".'

Under the Mosaic sacrificial law only unblemished animals were acceptable. If we accept the New Testament's account of Jesus, we are honour bound to see in Him and the cross, the fulfilment of that to which the sacrificial system pointed. Read Isaiah 53 for a graphic foreshadowing. If Jesus had been born naturally He would be blemished by Adam's sinful hereditary.

Christmas is Heaven's answer to the problem of the right to the throne: the fulfilment of God's curse on Jehoiakim: and the fitness of Jesus to be our redeemer.

Prayer: Life so often tries to annul your promises and purposes, beloved Lord. How the Darkness must have smiled its deathly smile when you cursed Jehoiakim and his son. We praise your Name, Eternal God, for you are never cornered or taken by surprise. Please help us to understand that when we feel hemmed in by life's difficulties.

My gift to you this day is my desire to understand your word in a deeper way so that I may unearth more of its 'hidden' richness.

Did The Angels Get It Wrong?

Day: 9

Reading: Luke 1:26-38

Every Christmas, that I can recall, emphasises the theme of peace on earth. If this is the angels' meaning it hasn't happened! Were they misguided in their enthusiasm? Did they misunderstand the reason for their song? Have we missed something?

My favourite Christmas hymn, *I Heard the Bells on Christmas Day* might hold a clue. Written by Henry W. Longfellow and J. Baptiste Calkin it has a verse: 'and in despair' I bowed my head: 'There is no peace on earth,' I said, 'for hate is strong, and mocks the song of peace on earth, good will to men.' It sums up succinctly the 'why' behind the absence of peace.

Did the birth of Jesus usher in the longed for promised reign of peace? Not so that anyone noticed. Perhaps the angels were making a long range promise. Maybe the angels were making a contrast between the Roman 'peace' and that promised by God of a covenant of peace. Rome imposed its 'peace' by military might. The Lord would provide peace but it would flow from within. A gift to receive, not something to impose.

Jesus is called the Prince of Peace!

Actually, He is a most disturbing person. His birth disturbed Herod and because of that Jerusalem trembled. Jesus is quoted in Matthew 10:34: 'Do not suppose that I have come to bring peace to the earth. I did not come to bring peace, but a sword.' He then goes on to show that when a person confessed Him as the Promised One he or she would find even their own family opposed to them. Why is this?

Simply because Jesus is not of this world! His values and purposes are at variance to the moral and spiritual ideals under the sway of the Devil in the kingdom of Darkness. Humankind's careless enjoyment of a sinful and materialistic lifestyle makes it deaf to coming judgement. It is also blind to the self-destructive consequences such behaviour sows. Christ makes people see and hear such unpleasant matters.

The angels were singing about something yet to be. Was it what Ezekiel foresaw and wrote in chapter 34: 24, 25 referring to a restored Israel: 'I the Lord will be their God and my servant David will be Prince among them. I the Lord have spoken. I will make a covenant of peace with them …'? Or what about Ezekiel 37:26-28: 'I will make a covenant of peace with them; it will be an everlasting covenant. I will establish them and increase their numbers, and I will put my sanctuary among them for ever. My dwelling place will be with them; I will be their God, and they will be my people. Then the nations will know that I the Lord make Israel holy, when my sanctuary is among them for ever.'

We know that Israel didn't warm to Jesus as King and Saviour. Many did, but not the leaders, even after the reality of the resurrection. Jesus could see this and was grieved by it. However, He also saw a time in the future when the nation would be brought to the inescapable realisation of who He is. 'You will not see me again until you say, 'Blessed is He who comes in the name of the Lord.' (Matthew 23:39).

The angels may also have been singing about a sign of God's pleasure in a person. All who understand they are accountable to the Holy and Righteous God have disquiet in their hearts and minds. They know they face a judgement day. No amount of self-hypnosis, that is, convincing yourself you are acceptable enough for God, or doing good works can deaden the anxiety. People know they can only be at peace with Him, and therefore, with themselves, if in grace and mercy He provided a way. Here is the more personal side of Christmas. The favour of God is bound up in the babe of the manger. God's peace revolved around Him. For men and women to find favour with the Eternal God meant they must have a relationship with Jesus, the Prince of Peace.

Christmas by itself could not do it. Christmas was the first earthly stage of providing the peace of God. This was achieved on the cross at Calvary! It is offered in the message, not of Christmas, but in the Gospel of the risen Lord. Personal peace is claimed when Jesus becomes Lord and Saviour. Peace is not a commodity, it is a person.

Prayer: Thank you, Jesus, for disturbing me and awakening me to my need of you as my Prince of Peace. I know I will face challenging times but I want to remain true to you. May your Word and your Spirit keep me abiding in your peace!

My gift to you today is to be an instrument so you can play your melody of peace in the midst of a chaotic and frantic environment.

The Magnificat – A Warrior's Song
Day: 10

Reading: Luke 1:46-56

The Magnificat, the title given to Mary's song, has the vibrancy of a warrior's faith. It has the sound of a victory march. Mary isn't a flaky pastry-type woman, beautiful but without substance. The brief pictures we have of her reveal a strong, even feisty woman, humble in her devotion; strong in her commitment to Yahweh and His purposes. As such she stands alongside other notable women who preceded her in the nation's history.

Among these women two stand out. One is Miriam, sister of Moses. After the rout of Pharaoh's army in the sea Moses bursts out in song (Exodus 15). Later Miriam joins in. She invites all to 'Sing to the Lord for He is highly exalted. The horse and its rider He has hurled into the sea.' Years later another woman comes on the scene. She leads the tribes, Zebulun and Naphtali, to victory over their enemies. Her name is Deborah. In Judges 5 is the song she sang in her triumph over Sisera. Mary's song links her to those brave women whose characters shine in Israel's history. Other women of note we could mention are Ruth, Hannah, and Esther. Unfortunately we don't have an account of any song they sang.

Luke 1:47: Mary is shown rejoicing in God her Saviour. The word 'rejoice' means to exult or leap for joy. It's used in Revelation 19:7 where a great multitude gathers at the marriage of the Lamb. It is a victory celebration.

Luke 1:49: Mary speaks of the Mighty One doing great things in her life. She must have been steeped in the writings of Isaiah, especially as her song echoes with his refrains. In the prophet's writing he likes to call Yahweh 'Saviour, Redeemer, Almighty.' These terms are often used in the context of a victorious contest (Isaiah 1:24. 49:26. 60:16).

Luke 1:51: The victory chant continues. The King James Authorised Version translates this verse, 'He has shown strength with His arm; He has scattered the proud in the imagination of their hearts.' The use of 'arm' Mary understood. Isaiah 52:10: 'The Lord will lay bare His holy arm in the sight of all the nations, and all the ends of the earth will see the salvation of our God.'

Was this young maiden also reassuring herself of His protection? Mary knew she would be the object of gossip, innuendoes, scorn and ridicule, not only from her neighbours, but from future generations of unbelievers. She trusted her Lord and Saviour to scatter their malicious thoughts and words. His purposes and her purity would prevail.

Luke 1:52 is not only a revisiting of history; it is a faith challenge to her era's dominant world power, Rome. The arrogant, immoral and worship-claiming Caesars would be brought down by the unpretentious, foot washing, leper touching Man from Galilee. Mary knew the Biblical principle that God resists the proud and exalts the humble.

In Luke 1:54, 55 the faithfulness of the Eternal God to His promises is emphasised. In-spite of the Nation's chequered history and abundant failures, the Almighty will fulfil His word to Israel. This should also be a great encouragement to us as we wait for Him to tie up the apparent loose ends of His promises to His Church. This also includes any promises He has given to you or me.

The faith of Mary was rooted and grounded in her conviction that God's Word was true. That's a conviction we have to arrive at personally. Without such confidence we will not make ourselves available to God as she did, when she called herself His 'bond servant.' Conviction leads to commitment, which, in turn, faces the injustices of life with faith, hope and love. Mary would need all of this, for she was told in Luke 2:34, 35 that Jesus would be a sign spoken against and that a 'sword will pierce your own soul too'.

Mary's warrior song was probably hummed many times as she confronted uncertain moments in Jesus' ministry. Was it 'playing' in the background of her tears at the cross? Did it burst with renewed strength at the resurrection? Will God bless us through her song today? Undoubtedly!

Prayer: Lord, I would repeat part of Mary's prayer as you call on me to be your servant, I am the Lord's servant, may it be to me as you have purposed.

My gift to you is to believe and obey your Word, not allowing difficulties to stagger me or personal likes and dislikes obstruct me.

The Herald of Christmas
Day: 11
Reading: Isaiah 40:1-8, Luke 3:67-79

Why does God do things the hard way? At least that's how we could view some of His actions! When reading the account in Luke about Zechariah and Elizabeth we can see a parallel with Abraham and Sarah's experience. I wonder how both couples felt about the ways of God? Surely Isaiah 55:8, 9 is an understatement. '"For my thoughts are not your thoughts, neither are my ways your ways," declares the Lord. "As the heavens are higher than the earth, so are my ways higher than your ways and my thoughts than your thoughts.".'

God's imposed silence on Zechariah may illustrate why God does things 'the hard way'. This is sensed in the response of the well wishers when the silence was broken. 'The neighbours were all filled with awe, and throughout the hill country of Judea people were talking about all these things' (Luke 1:65). Who received the praise? The Lord, the God of Israel. This was and ever would be His approach. Why? So that no one could boast as though they had achieved the impossible!

The baby, John, was to be the preparer of the way for the Messiah. Zechariah's song is also a prophecy of the role his child was to undertake. 'You, my child, will be called a prophet of the Most High; for you will go on before the Lord to prepare the way for Him, to give His people the knowledge of salvation through the forgiveness of their sins …' (Luke 1:76, 77).

The man from the wilderness burst upon the religious and political scene like a tornado. His preaching aroused men and women to faith in God. People were stirred to ask what he, John, was doing and why. John left them in no doubt. He wasn't the expected prophet. He wasn't the Promised One. He was a voice calling in the wilderness, 'Make straight paths for Him' – the Promised One.

One of the beautiful things about John is his readiness to honour Jesus. What he said in John 3:29, 30, has implications for us also. 'The bride belongs to the bridegroom. The friend who attends the bridegroom waits and listens for him, and is full of joy when he hears the bridegroom's voice. That joy is mine, and is now complete. He must become greater; I must become less.'

Whilst his ministry was and remains unique, it is also a metaphor for every Christian's role. We must prepare the way. We need to make it easier for men and women to have an encounter with the Christ, the Lord of Glory. There is always a lot of emotional, historical and relational rubble causing a barrier between a person and a meeting with Jesus. We are called upon to try and clear that rubble with wisdom, patience and faithfulness. God places His people in the face of such obstacles as ignorance, false teaching, hurts and self loathing. We are to be His 'road builders and rubble clearers'. Many times we will wonder if our labour is worthwhile. Any response seems minimal at best, non-existent at worst. However, be encouraged by Isaiah 55:10, 11: 'As the rain and the snow come down from heaven, and do not return to it without watering the earth and making it bud and flourish, so that it yields seed for the sower and bread for the eater, so is my word that goes out from my mouth. It will not return to me empty, but will accomplish what I desire and achieve the purpose for which I sent it.'

John was also a 'signpost' pointing to Jesus as the Lamb of God. The One born on an unknown day we call Christmas is the Saviour of the World. We are not 'signposts' to Jesus merely being a nice man, an excellent teacher or a miracle worker. We have a more important message to get across. Jesus is the Lamb of God, the One who fulfils the plan God wove in the ritual of the Jewish tabernacle and the animal sacrifices.

Isaiah 40 opens with the wonderful words 'Comfort, comfort my people'. Christmas is God's desire to comfort His people whilst at the same time doing battle with His enemies. When we enlist in the company of Christ's disciples we are to embrace both facets of the calling. This was John's privilege. It is also ours!

Prayer: There are so many, Eternal God, who are hurting, especially at Christmas time. I would pray that they will know your comfort and your forgiveness. If it is possible, may I be a 'road mender' into their lives.

My gift to you today would be to allow you to make me your 'preparer of the way' in my household and community.

Christmas Expresses God's Heart
Day: 12

Reading: John 3:1-19

'Bah humbug' was Scrooge's response to the sounds of Christmas in Charles Dickens' famous story, *A Christmas Carol*. In many ways, I've sympathy for Scrooge, for the way Christmas is celebrated and viewed in the light of the Gospels, Scrooge is right!

Looking at Christmas in isolation from other events is to simply get warm and fuzzy feelings over a babe in a manger. A baby is defenceless and dependent and, therefore, not threatening. You can't say the same about the Man with the scars of the Cross. Christmas isn't about cards, parties, carols and lighting candles or praying for peace. The manger is a challenge from God in the form of the One who would grow to shake societies across the centuries. The early Church wasn't caught up in the celebration of Christmas. Its euphoria was in celebrating God's eternal grace as displayed in the message of the Cross.

Christmas is Heaven's love gift to Earth. 'For God so loved the world that He gave His one and only Son, that whoever believes in Him shall not perish but have eternal life.' The identity of this 'one and only Son' is finger-printed in John 3:13: 'No one has ever gone into heaven except the one who came from heaven – the Son of Man.' This title is a prophetic one. Constantly in the Gospels it is claimed by Jesus for Himself.

How did He come down from heaven? Not in a chariot! Not as a spectator! Not as a spy! He came to fulfil a unique and promised mission. His coming expressed the heart of God towards men and women. Described as prisoners in the realm of darkness, slaves of sin and playthings of death and the Devil, humanity was in need of a Saviour.

As in any conflict, the enemy seeks to smear the intent and integrity of their opposition. The realm of darkness has a ready made press and a sympathetic audience for its slander of the Holy and Righteous God. He is accused of indifference, weakness, hatred of His creation, or a bigot because of ongoing injustices, calamities and disease. When looking at this violent, corrupt and despairing world, such thinking seems logical and, therefore, acceptable and self-justifying. Christmas and Easter – as indeed the scriptures from Genesis to Revelation – refute that assertion. The cradle and the cross continue to tell us that God isn't indifferent or ignorant of humankind's situation. The Lord God did not cause the problem. He did, however, accept responsibility for putting things right

In the Old Testament there is a book of tears and heartbreak. From the first words to the last, sorrow flows like a waterfall from a faithful man over the destruction of his country and city. He knew the nation had reaped the consequences of its actions and unbelief. Looking on the rubble Jeremiah must have wondered, even if for a fleeting moment, where was God in all this, what of His promises? In what must be one of the most remarkable and faith gripping passages in Scripture, Jeremiah declares the faithfulness of God.

'I remember my affliction and my wandering, the bitterness and the gall. I well remember them, and my soul is downcast within me. Yet this I call to mind and therefore I have hope: Because of the Lord's great love we are not consumed, for His Compassions never fail. They are new every morning; great is your faithfulness. I say to myself, "The Lord is my portion; therefore I will wait for Him."' (Lamentations 3:19-24).

Unless unfailing love and unmerited mercy is seen being offered within Christmas to a sad, needy and cursed world, any of us will sentimentalise it, debase it or see it as 'Bah humbug'! The Christmas option is before us. 'Whoever believes in Him is not condemned, but whoever does not believe stands condemned already because he has not believed in the name of God's one and only Son.' (John3:18).

Prayer: Darkness melts away in the light of your Word, beloved Lord. The tendency of my heart to use Christmas for personal gain and make this Christ event 'humbug' is held in check as I taste your love and mercy. Thank you Lord for opening my eyes to your love!

My gift to you this Christmas will be to assist people overcome the 'Scrooge' mentality by pointing to the manger through the 'lens' of the cross.

Behold Your Salvation
Day: 13

Readings: Luke 2:25-35, Matthew 1:21

The drowning man floundering around in the water knows his own helplessness. He needs a life-saver. His desperate prayer is for someone to see his plight and send a rescuer. No sense of drowning, no need for a life-saver!

The Bible informs us that, in God's eyes, the world is drowning in wickedness. Few, however, seem to believe it or care. Still, the Lord God sent His Son on a rescue mission to save those who recognised their need and called out for help. Paul says in Romans 10:12, 13: 'There is no difference between Jew and Gentile – the same Lord is Lord of all and richly blesses all who call on Him, for, 'Everyone who calls upon the Name of the Lord will be saved.''

When we call Jesus 'Saviour and Lord' we are faced with a Biblical dilemma. In Hosea 13:4 the prophet quotes God as saying, 'I am the Lord your God ... You shall acknowledge no God but me, no saviour except me.' Over and over again, Yahweh is viewed in Scripture as Saviour. As such, He requires people to recognise that fact and to worship only Him. 'I, even I, am the Lord, and apart from me there is no saviour.' (Isaiah 43:11, compare 45:21).

When the angel announced to Joseph the news of Mary's pregnancy, the angel also indicated the baby's name and mission – 'He shall save his people from their sins'. Does this mean that Yahweh has sub-let His salvation prerogative? Unlikely! Was the given name – Joshua in Hebrew, Jesus in the Greek – merely a name tag for identification purposes? Surely, it points to something far more meaningful, something far greater. Put the name along side the name Emmanuel and surely you sense something wonderful. 'The Lord saves, God is with us'.

Holding a promise in his heart and mind, an old man hovered around the precincts of the Temple. He was convinced that God had told him he would not die until his eyes had seen the One who would be the Messiah.

When Mary and Joseph came forty-one days after the birth to fulfil the purification ritual, old Simeon was there. Was he expecting a baby? Was he looking for an Old Testament warrior judge? Whatever his expectations, when he saw the baby he knew his hope had been fulfilled. 'This is the Messiah!' Simeon declared. Did Mary and Joseph react to this old man taking the child Jesus in his arms and rejoicing in the Lord before them? Did they say 'amen!' to his words? I wonder.

Four remarkable comments are made by this saint of God.

1st 'My eyes have seen your salvation'. A baby is the Saviour?! Any bystanders must have felt sorry for him or embarrassed by such a statement. However, he had pierced time and grasped the baby's future.

2nd 'Which you have prepared in the sight of all the people'. Christmas is not a secret. It doesn't belong to a special class or group of people. This event may have been long in coming, but it was well documented.

3rd 'A light for revelation to the Gentiles'. This would have shaken the Pharisee's understanding that Gentiles were fodder for wrath. God had not forgotten the descendents of Japheth and Ham. Those nations longed for a Saviour and knowledge of God, although their longings were devoid of hope. Jesus would offer them Heaven's unfailing light of grace, truth, love and hope.

4th Simeon saw in the baby 'the glory of your people Israel'. How could this be? Today Jesus is anathema to the descendents of Abraham, Isaac and Jacob, mainly due to the horrors inflicted on them by so called Christians. Jesus is their glory, unrecognised at this moment, but foretold that He will be in their future. Romans 11:26, 27: 'The deliverer will come from Zion; He will turn godlessness away from Jacob. And this is my covenant with them when I take away their sins' Why? 'For God's gifts and His call are irrevocable' (Romans 11:29).

My prayer: May Simeon's embrace of the Babe and his statements continue to find their fulfilment in the story of Jesus at Christmas, and all the year round.

My gift to you would be to lift high your light to the Gentiles, and help the Jewish people see Jesus as their glory.

A Body Prepared
Day: 14
Reading: Hebrews 10:1-10, 2:5-9

Since World War II there has been a remembrance time on June 6th to re-emphasise the importance of D-Day. That began the overthrow of Hitler's regime. Christmas is the spiritual equivalent of D-Day. It is the commemoration of the Heavenly invasion in the person of Jesus. There will ever only be one Christmas. We celebrate that event continuously with pleasure as Christians. To us, it isn't a mindless carnival. It's a reminder of the historic 'beach head' Heaven made in its reclaiming of creation.

Whilst we know the exact date of D-Day we have no way of knowing the date of Christ's coming into this world. The 25th of December was chosen for political reasons rather than factual. In the scheme of salvation the date doesn't matter. We know for certain the date, place and time of the crucifixion and resurrection. That is the crucial issue on which to build our lives and destiny.

Why then, was it important for Jesus to be born the way He was? Our reading highlights one of many reasons. In the context it is plain to see the relationship between His body and the various animal sacrifices ritually performed in the Jewish worship. The animals used in sacrifice had to meet strict requirements. Any deformity, blemish or illness made them unfit to be offered. They were debarred by the Mosaic Law. Unblemished after investigation however guaranteed acceptance. If Jesus had been conceived through the union of Joseph and Mary, He would have been blemished, as are all descendents of Adam. This is why the body of Jesus is no hit or miss affair. It's 'a body prepared'!

For Jesus, Christmas began Thirty-three years of living under the intense scrutiny of Heaven, the powers of darkness, the religious groupings of Judaism, the scepticism of the Gentiles, and the familiarity of family and friends. Hebrews 5:8, 9: 'Although He was a son, He learnt obedience from what He suffered and once made perfect, He became the source of eternal salvation to all who obey Him.' The perfection talked about was not referring to His person. It pointed to His performance, to His unblemished behaviour, attitude and relationships. That is why at His trial He could ask if there was anyone able to throw up any sin in His life. The letters in the New Testament uphold the sinless nature of Jesus. He met the requirements of the Old Testament Mosaic Law and thereby fulfilled all righteousness.

Why did God go to such great lengths to ensure that the Promised One's body should meet these unbending standards? Only the Bible can answer that. God is the supreme perfectionist and requires that His standard is met. We want Him to bend the rules in our favour because we know our imperfections. However, He is the measure, the standard to meet. We have to meet Him on His terms or we'll not abide in His presence (Matthew 5:48). This also applied to Jesus. He measured up! We don't! Therefore, if we are to have fellowship with our Creator and Sovereign, we need someone who will make us as Jesus in the Father's eyes. That means dealing with our personal sin and our inheritance from Adam. Jesus did that on the cross as our substitute. He paid the wages of Sin (Romans 6:23). More than that, Jesus bestowed upon us His Righteousness when, by the obedience of faith, we ask Him to be our Saviour and Lord. (Galatians 3:26, 27). Another reason we need to belong to Jesus in the Father's eyes is due to the fact that we are accident prone in moral, spiritual, intellectual and emotional areas of life. Jesus needed to become our advocate, our High Priest, who understands us, sympathises with us, prays for us, stands with us and pleads our case for forgiveness through our repentance. Read Hebrews 2:14-18, 4:14-16.

Christmas began this. The Cross made it achievable. The resurrection made it a reality. Faith on our part releases His unblemished life and victory into our lives.

The crucified body of Jesus was put in a tomb. When He rose bodily as conqueror, Jesus had a glorified body untouchable by time or space, death or decay. He was touched. He ate. He fellowshipped, and the nail and spear prints were visible and they guarantee His authenticity. The wonder of our future is that we too, will receive a similar body when our lives have run their race here on earth. (Philippians 3:21). However, we will not have the scars.

Prayer: It is beyond my understanding, Lord Jesus, why you would clothe yourself in the likeness of sinful flesh for a person such as I? I fall at your feet in adoration and ask for an ever increasing understanding of the wonder of 'a body prepared'. Amen!

My gift to you is tattered, torn and worn but maybe you can do something with it. Let my body be your workshop and launching pad to make who you are and what you have done known in my sphere of influence.

The Time Has Arrived

Day: 15

Reading: Galatians 4:1-7

If Heaven had a clock, we on earth would think there were times it was slow or even stopped. God is outside our time frame and yet operates within it for our benefit and instruction. In the reading, Paul stresses the arrival of the birth of Jesus was in the fullness of time. There is more meaning to this than God simply finding the right woman to bear the Messiah.

The Christian Faith is interwoven in history. Its view on history is a remarkable feature which differentiates the Judeo/Christian Faith from all others! God has put His integrity and His Word in the critics' den for them to wrestle with. Every time they imagine they've found a flaw in God's Word they end up conceding their error, however reluctantly.

When Paul talks about 'Christmas' arriving when the time was ripe he had an historical framework in mind. Secular and sacred history came together as foretold by Daniel. He had been called upon to interpret Nebuchadnezzar's dream (Daniel 2) concerning four world empires. The third kingdom referred to Alexander the Great, who established Greek supremacy over the regions of the Middle East and the Mediterranean. In so doing, he made Greek the language of trade and commerce. The fourth world power referred to is Rome. We are well aware of their genius in building roads, bridges and monuments. These two kingdoms were used by God to facilitate the coming of Jesus and the propagation of His life, ministry, teaching, death and resurrection. The translation of the Old Testament (Jesus' Bible) into the Greek tongue dispersed the knowledge of and expectations for a Messiah who was promised to the world through the Jewish religion. History knows it as the 'Septuagint'. This was also the first attempt to translate the Hebrew Scriptures into another language. This became the Bible of most of the New Testament writers.

Luke, as an historian of repute, links the birth of Jesus to the reign of Caesar Augustus and the governor of Syria, Quirinius (Luke 2:1-3). This gives us a time frame in which to work. However, there may be more to Luke's intention than that. Is it possible Luke, consciously or unconsciously, is saying that the real ruler of the World, the Lord of lords and King of kings had appeared? Here is a direct challenge to the Roman Caesars self deification and their subjects' emperor worship. Here is a contest in the making. Who is Lord? Will the Babe of Bethlehem, the future crucified One, command the allegiance of all or will the corrupt power of a Caesar prevail?

Reading Daniel 9:20-27 makes us aware of another specific time frame. From the rebuilding of Jerusalem after the Babylonian captivity to the coming of the Anointed One (the Messiah) and His subsequent 'cutting off' would cover 483 years. We know this 'cutting off' pointed to the cross. Therefore 33 years earlier the Anointed One came in the fullness of time. The Apostle Paul, well versed in his scriptures, probably had in mind the features Daniel wrote about as preceding and preparing the way for the Son of Man. The Old Testament pointed to the tribe to which the Messiah belonged, to His unique birth and birth place, to His character and various features of His ministry and suffering. What wasn't spelled out was the date. Writing to the Galatians, the apostle Paul sums it up very well. He may well have amplified it when he was previously with them in person.

'God sent His Son …' means being commissioned to fulfil a mission. The Eternal Word came into the world as the Apostle of the Father. His task is multi-faceted. Redeeming men and women from sin's slavery, destroying the Evil triumvirate of sin, death and Satan, fulfilling the Mosaic Law, being a Light to the Gentiles and establishing the Kingdom of God are all in His 'job' description. Jesus had to be born 'under the Law' for it would be this Law which would be used against Him. In turn, this Law would vindicate Him. This is the testimony of the resurrection. Without Christmas there could be no 'Mission begun'.

The conviction under-girding the 'fullness of time' is also our grounds for optimism for those future events promised in the Scriptures. They may seem to tarry and we may wait impatiently, but they will take place according to God's calendar in the fullness of time.

Prayer: Almighty God, grant us the patience to wait in faith, hope and love for you to fulfil your word. May we have an appreciation of the way you merge secular and sacred history to meet at the right time and place to fulfil your purposes.

My gift to you is to hang up my personal calendar and accept what you do and the time you choose to do it. I'll learn to wait and persevere until your time is ripe.

Christmas – When God Arrived
Day: 16

Reading: John 1:1-14

Our body is sometimes described as a 'tent' by New Testament writers. We live within it in an intimate and dependent manner, but one day we will put it aside. We understand it is fragile and ultimately will return to its kindred elements. Rather than be overwhelmed by such a gloomy outlook, the Bible points to a more glorious and eternal body which is promised to the disciples of Christ (2 Corinthians 5:1-5, 2 Peter 1:12-15).

Christmas is a time to remember that God in Christ Jesus clothed Himself with the 'tent' of our temporary bodily existence. The apostle John is very particular in using the word translated as 'dwelling among us'. It has a long Old Testament history as the word 'Tabernacle'.

As you read the books of Exodus, Leviticus, Numbers and Deuteronomy, it is evident that the Lord God desired to dwell in the midst of His people. He wanted to be their focal point as well as their guardian. To do this, a simple, yet beautiful, mobile worship centre called the Tabernacle was constructed. When Israel camped the tabernacle was situated in the centre of the people. When they journeyed, the Tabernacle was in the middle of the marchers. To approach the Tabernacle required prescribed sacrifices and a specific priesthood. This gracious arrangement was ultimately contaminated by the wickedness of unbelief, disobedience and idolatry. God withdrew from His dwelling place, reluctantly, though deliberately, as noted in Ezekiel 8 to 11.

His going didn't remove His desire to be with His people, but how could He be with them – especially when, after the destruction of the first temple in Jerusalem, He never took up residence in the second temple? (Compare Ezekiel chapters 10 - 11:22. He will not enter the next temple until Christ returns as promised). The second temple was built under Ezra, and was beautifully refurbished by King Herod. In 'tabernacling' in human flesh, God expressed His desire for fellowship with us. He also came to make it possible for us to measure up to His requirements for such fellowship (Romans 3:23. 8:1-4).

John, in his expressive and challenging manner, tells the Christmas story from a unique angle. In doing so, he gives us precious insights into the person of the One who came. 'In the beginning was the Word ...' Here we are, taken back to Genesis chapter one. Creation began with God's Word. He spoke – it happened! When John uses the Greek term *logos* for Word, he is expressing a wonderful spiritual and philosophical truth. The One he is writing about was there at the beginning of creation. He is the creator. This Logos is God and it is He who has come to earth. For a devout Jewish man to write such a statement required a dramatic, overwhelming conviction and an ability to justify his thinking from the Scriptures! There is much to say on this, and Matthew 28:19, 20 would sum up the wonder of the Christian understanding of the Godhead: '... make disciples of all nations, baptising them in *the Name* of the Father and of the Son and of the Holy Spirit ...' (emphasis added). One Name, one essence, expressed in three personalities (John 10:30) (Genesis 1:26). Throughout his Gospel John stresses the wonder of the Word becoming flesh.

Two other words are used to describe Jesus: Light and Life. He didn't reflect the Light of God, He *is* that Light. He didn't gain life as we do, by conception. There was never a time when He and Life were separate. When Jesus walked this earth there was something appealing about Him, perhaps unexplainable, yet arresting. Would this uncreated beauty have been recognised as He lay in the manger? Were the shepherds overawed by Him? When the Magi arrived, why would they have bowed down and worshipped Him if there wasn't the awareness of something awesome about this child?

Christmas is God's last endeavour to tabernacle with Humanity so He can lead them into an eternal relationship with Himself. Hebrews 1:1-3: 'In the past God spoke to our forefathers through the prophets at many times and in various ways, but in these last days he has spoken to us by his Son, who he appointed heir of all things, and through whom he made the universe. The Son is the radiance of God's glory and the exact representation of his being, sustaining all things by His powerful word. After He had provided purification for sins, He sat down at the right hand of the Majesty in heaven.'

Prayer: You must have been beautiful to behold as a babe and as a man. How graphic then, Beloved Lord, is the scriptures which depict you on the cross as marred hideously and beyond description. You became that for me, so that my sin and treason could be dealt with. I bow in adoration before you.

My gift to you is this tabernacle in which I live and move, that you will have sovereign claim to it now and forever.

Christmas in Contrast
Day: 17

Reading: 2 Corinthians 8:1-9

When I was growing up there was a Christmas custom whereby we gave the milkman, the garbage collectors and the postman a small gift. This was a thank you for their labours through the year. Of course, much of that personal interaction has gone today. We did it then, in the words of our reading, from enjoying the 'grace of giving'.

Why is there a sense that the Christmas event, as far as the majority are concerned, is a time for giving? How could you explain why men and women, especially on Christmas day, give up their time and family enjoyments to serve the more unfortunate people of the community? Again we refer to our text and understand the reason to be in the example of Jesus. 'For you know the grace of our Lord Jesus Christ that though He was rich, yet for your sakes He became poor, so that you through His poverty might become rich.'

Here is the contrast of Christmas. Jesus left behind the riches of glory to become the child of a peasant carpenter family in an obscure village called Nazareth. He who is the Lord of Host with legions of angels to command became a Rabbi to uncouth fishermen and outcasts of society. He who was worshipped in the Heavenly realms was despised and rejected on the earth He had created. People Jesus had breathed life into through the creative act of Adam now breathed abuse and unbelief at Him. This Jesus put aside the splendour of Heaven to tramp the countryside of Israel without a permanent place to rest His head. He warned would be followers a similar experience could well be theirs. A person would have to be utterly convinced that Jesus was and is the One promised by Scripture to take up His invitation to join Him. This is especially so after He was humiliated and put to death on a cross.

How then, has He made us rich? On the surface He doesn't have much going for Him as He seeks to enlist disciples. This is why, if you think in monetary terms, you have missed the mark. The answer is summed up in Ephesians 1:3: 'Praise be to the God and Father of our Lord Jesus Christ, who has blessed us in the heavenly realms with every spiritual blessing in Christ.' This letter probably offers us an understanding of our riches more than any other scripture. It is worth reading and underlining the treasures we possess, treasures that persecution, sickness, poverty, theft and even death, cannot steal. By faith in Jesus Christ as Lord and Saviour, we have been adopted into God's family. This means we have received redemption, forgiveness, an understanding of God's purposes. It also includes an eternal inheritance, His presence, power and providence, citizenship in Heaven, and Christ in us.

These are God's gems of glory which never fade or wear away. None of these are available outside of Christ Jesus. Therefore, we can truly say, regardless of physical circumstances, we are the richest of all people. In gratitude we bow before our heavenly Father and say, 'Thanks be to God for His indescribable gift!' (2 Corinthians 9:15).

May we never lose sight of the wonder of He who possesses us so that we may possess these riches! We should stand in amazement at God's trust in us, for we know our frailties and follies. We are, in Biblical terms, 'earthen vessels'! God must enjoy such pottery. Why? 2 Corinthians 4:6-7: 'For God, who said, let light shine out of darkness, made his light shine in our hearts to give the light of the knowledge of God's glory displayed in the face of Christ. But we have this treasure in jars of clay to show that this all-surpassing power is from God and not from us.'

Prayer: As you have been so gracious in what you have given to me, beloved Lord, may my desire be to honour you in the way I express your richness in me to others.

My gift to Jesus is those areas of my inner poverty and selfish outlook so that He will transform them. I desire to honour Him by accepting, expressing and sharing the riches of His grace.

Emmanuel

Day: 18

Reading: Isaiah 7:14, Matthew 1:18-25

It's party time! Come on, let's celebrate! However, it's hard to celebrate any event on your own and Christmas is a time for celebrating. Good company, safe surroundings and adequate food are some of the highlights of Christmas. Having family and friends around makes for a great day! As with other celebrations that centre around someone's achievements, the enjoyment increases the better you know the guest of honour. The same applies to Christmas. I wonder how many would be embarrassed if the Christmas Celebrity turned up to the festivities ostensibly held in His honour?

In His earthly life Jesus seemed to enjoy company. Throughout the Gospels are stories of Him sharing in meal times and, of course, the Passover celebration. I like the fact that Jesus had the pride of place at Matthew's house. This tax collector had called the party to make an announcement. Imagine their stunned looks when he told his taxation friends and others of becoming an unemployed disciple of Jesus.

Often we look on Christmas as a time to enjoy presents, holidays and carolling, etc. For those who have a spiritual insight into Christmas it comes as no surprise that God enjoys this time also. He is the God who loves company. Strange as it may sound, He appreciates being with the descendants of Adam and Eve. In the Genesis account of the Creation we read the story of God 'walking' in the Garden of Eden to have some time with Adam and Eve.

Because Adam's treason shattered this 'walking in the garden' relationship we may also have a sense of loss, that is undefinable yet real. God may be for many the unknown Creator, yet within their hearts there is a longing to meet Him. As understandable as this is, have we ever considered the other side? Do we think of the loss the Eternal God must have felt as He was unable to enjoy the company of those He loved? Would He also have missed their reciprocal love?

When reading the thrilling story of Moses and the Exodus, especially the Nation's journey through the wilderness, there is a feature that is often overlooked. In the midst of their orderly, systematic marching is the symbol of the presence of Yahweh. The Ark of the Covenant expressed the heart of God's fellowship with His people.

Emmanuel is more than a name for Jesus. It's a statement of the desire of God. We know what it means – God with us – but do we believe it? Christmas is His movement towards those who have run away from Him. In the Bethlehem event God stepped into His creation with a plan to restore the broken relationship. There may well be a desire in our hearts for God, but unless He can mend the breech we will remain separated.

Emmanuel is more than a sentimental concept. Woven into it are promises from the God who never lies, with guarantees from the One who signed them with His own blood. There is always a cost in restoring fractured friendships. In the case of God and us, the cost was beyond us. Restoration required resurrection life. That is a new beginning where the realm of Adam gives way to the Headship of Jesus (2 Corinthians 5:17). God could not simply reach down. He had to come down to lead us out of one realm into the other.

To call Jesus Emmanuel is to make known the wonder of an amazing privilege. God has chosen to join our ranks, experience our pain first hand, stand with us in our struggles, share with us His resources so as to carry the load, withstand the 'storm', and to be at peace in the midst of uncertainties.

Christmas, for us, can be a celebration of God coming to be with us, then calling us to walk with Him in a faith relationship. In a sense, this time of the year makes Psalm 23 a song of our journey. Emmanuel is our Shepherd. He has come to lead us through life's varying experiences to an assured place in His presence. His call to follow Him is bound up in the message of the good news of the Easter event. We respond by conviction of its truth, surrender to its claim and live it out by faith. His promise is that one day we shall see Him face to face. That's the goal of Christmas! Now that *is* something to celebrate!

Prayer: Lord, there are times when I doubt or forget your companionship because life's pressures and struggles cloud you out. Forgive me please and help me to trust in the wonder of your Name, Emmanuel, which reminds me that you will always be with me.

My gift to you is a desire to have fellowship with you in deeper and more meaningful ways. Be the centre of my life and sovereign over all I am and have.

From What Does Christ Save Us?
Day: 19

Reading: 1 Timothy 1:12-18

In the reading the apostle Paul stresses the reason Christ Jesus came was to save sinners. He was thankful, as he considered himself the foremost of those who missed God's standard. However, he does not spell out what sinners have been saved from. We almost automatically think of salvation from judgement, death and the power of Satan. True, but it isn't the whole reason. Maybe there is a more pressing reason which surpasses all others.

I would suggest the main purpose for our salvation was to save us from God Himself. Why? Surely God is love! Love undergirds Christmas and Calvary. Right? But what does Deuteronomy 4:24 say? 'The Lord your God is a consuming fire, a jealous God.' Some may be tempted to relegate that to an Old Testament concept, but Hebrews 12:29 quotes it and warns against treating Him lightly.

This presentation of God must refer to His holiness which blazes against all wickedness, self enthronement and counterfeit goodness. The Ten Commandments expressed the Lord's unchanging standards. When we stand beneath their searchlight they show how far we have fallen short. We cannot deny we have violated His Law. We are not only condemned but in His presence the clothing of our soul is revealed for what it is. Isaiah 64:6: 'All of us have become like one who is unclean, and all our righteous acts are like filthy rags; we all shrivel up like a leaf, and like the wind our sins sweep us away.' One day we will have to stand before Him, what a frightful prospect if we had to stand alone.

Christmas is our Lord coming to earth to satisfy the wrath of the Father. Some may find this unpalatable, but scripture reminds us that God is angry with His creation every minute of every day. A day of accounting has been fixed. God knows the time, we don't. The Lord God has provided Jesus to satisfy the demands of holy righteousness and judicial wrath. It's an atoning sacrifice, according to 1 John 2:2. Jesus also provided a proper covering for people to stand in the Father's presence! When we accept Jesus as our redeemer He clothes us in His righteousness. Not only that, He promises to stand with us when it is time to appear before the Father's throne. None of this applies to the person who dismisses Jesus as unnecessary to being accepted by God.

Believers in Jesus Christ still have to give an account of their life and service before the Father. 1 Corinthians 3:11-15: 'No one can lay any foundation other than the one already laid, which is Jesus Christ. If anyone builds on this foundation using gold, silver, costly stones, wood, hay or straw, their work will be shown for what it is because the Day will bring it to light. It will be revealed with fire, and the fire will test the quality of each person's work. If what has been built survives, the builder will receive a reward. If it is burnt up, the builder will suffer loss but yet will be saved – even though only as one escaping through the flames.'

Christmas linked with Easter means we do not have to dread meeting the eternal God in His capacity as judge. We have become 'family', according to John 1:12-13. Now we can honestly, joyfully, humbly say 'our Father' to Him who dwells in the consuming radiance of holiness. John 17:24: 'Father, I want those you have given me to be with me where I am, and to see my glory, the glory you have given me because you loved me before the creation of the world.' Jesus is our security. He is our Covering. He is our guarantor.

Prayer: Beloved Lord, thank you for coming into my life and providing me with a safe place from the fire of judgement and clothing me in garments acceptable in Glory.

My gift to the Lord Jesus is my desire to live out daily what you have bestowed within. I want to uphold the holiness of my God in the everyday affairs of living.

'The Light of Life'
Day: 20

Reading: John 10:1-10

'I have come that they may have life, and have it to the full.' John 10:10.

Robbers and thieves enjoy Christmas. For them it's a profitable time, due to people's carelessness about security. Religion has its thieves and robbers too. In fact, Jesus takes the analogy even further. He calls them murderers and destroyers. Who are the predators? False teachers and ministers addicted to money. History is filled with people who not only 'fleece the sheep', they also defame the name and integrity of the eternal Lord God. His wrath and judgement is their destiny.

In contrast to these agents of evil, Jesus didn't come to take. He came to give so His people would have a full and overflowing life. Such an offer will only be understood through Biblical lenses. The Bible tells us that men and women are alienated from God spiritually, describing them as dead. This doesn't appeal to humankind's ego, for it considers itself alive and well. Jesus describes His view of life differently.

In John 17 we come to realise that 'Life' is a relationship with God as the Father and Jesus as the Christ. Knowing goes beyond the intellectual into the commitment realm. Paul says, 'Set your minds on things above, not on earthly things. For you died and your life is now hidden with Christ in God. When Christ, who is your life, appears, then you also will appear with Him in glory' Colossians 3:2-3. Notice what Jesus was offering in John 10:10? Himself!

Jesus Christ offers many things to us. Here are a few: freedom from the power and penalty of sin, the joy of forgiveness, hope despite seemingly hopeless circumstances, and the promise of a new destiny with Jesus and seeing His glory. Also, nothing can separate Him from His people.

Another facet of what Jesus offers is in John 12:46: 'I have come into the world as a light, so that no one who believes in me should stay in darkness.' What is the darkness He mentions? Primarily, it refers to the realm of the prince of this world – a state in which the knowledge of the Lord God of Glory is resisted, His Law ridiculed, and His call to newness of life opposed. Christ Jesus is a ray of light that penetrates this darkness. Those who long for the light of life and are willing to leave the darkness will find the truth of John 8:12: 'I am the light of the world. Whoever follows me will never walk in darkness, but will have the light of life.'

Take Jesus and His word out of the world and what is left? Darkness! Lifelessness! This would rule a person's domain. Unless the Eternal made Himself known, no amount of searching could find Him. Christmas is therefore a declaration of God unveiling Himself. He set out on a rescue mission at great personal cost and humiliation to introduce Himself to those on this prodigal planet. The cross was the final, desperate attempt to crush 'the Light'. What happened? Light was transformed into the 'rainbow of grace'. Regardless of your sin, despair, trauma and occult bondage, Christ as the crucified light has a grace 'colour' suitable to give you new, abundant, eternal life!

The Christmas light is not the decoration of tree or house. It is the spiritual aurora of the Babe of Bethlehem, the Man of Nazareth, the risen Lord Jesus! He alone lights up your life with spiritual understanding, heavenly anticipation, holy integrity and protection from the wiles of the ungodly! He does this by His indwelling presence and the unleashing of His written word. The aged Simeon understood this as he held the Christ child in the temple courts. Luke 2:30-32: 'My eyes have seen your salvation, which you have prepared in the sight of all nations: a light for revelation to the Gentiles and the glory of your people Israel.'

Prayer: Heavenly Father, I'm humbled by your efforts to seek and save me from temporal as well as eternal Darkness. I bow before you in awe of the Life you have offered me in Christ Jesus. Amen.

My gift to the Lord Jesus is a desire to know and understand what it means to be His light in this dark world.

Choices Jesus Made
Day: 21
Reading: Philippians 2:5-11

Christmas shopping can make a person neurotic. Making choices, weighing up prices and expectations whilst watching the bank balance is tiring! We can only hope that those receiving the gifts appreciate what has been given.

Do we appreciate the gifts of grace we have received from Jesus? Our Lord paid an extravagant price to make them available to us, a price none of us could ever afford! Our reading highlights the cost Jesus paid in His desire to offer you something money cannot buy.

The Lord of Glory 'made Himself nothing' when He chose to make Christmas a reality. Notice that no one made Him nothing. It was a deliberate and personal decision. This emptying is explained in this passage. It was also lived out in His life, as recorded in the Gospels. The Lord did not give up His deity. He clothed Himself in the humanity of Adam's descendents with a notable difference. Jesus did not carry the inherited Sin nature from Adam. This is one of the reasons for the virgin birth. When you read the New Testament you will find an awareness of the divine and the human nature of Jesus. However, in His humanity Jesus never resorted to using His divinity. What Jesus did, He did as the expression of the Second Adam under the authority of His heavenly Father. Jesus is quoted in John 5:19: 'Very truly I tell you, the Son can do nothing by himself; he can do only what he sees his Father doing, because whatever the Father does the Son also does.' It was also done in the power of the indwelling Holy Spirit. Any other approach to this earthly life would have cancelled Him out as our example, advocate, Saviour.

If I had a choice of leaving our realm for some other, how would I plan my arrival and reception? I would probably place myself in a royal household, or as an aristocratic or famous celebrity. Something in us recoils from the choice Jesus made – that is, becoming a servant. More than a mere servant, the Biblical word points to a bond slave without any protection in law.

As if that wasn't bad enough, Jesus came to redeem men and women from the power, penalty and possession of sin through His death on a cross.

Christmas was a death sentence in the making. For salvation required paying the penalty incurred by sin and rebellion against God's person, word and creation (Romans 6:23). Now, our Lord could have chosen to limit Himself to some fashionable status and come to earth as a nobleman, a successful businessman or artisan. He could have chosen to die as a warrior or a hero. He didn't! Jesus was born into a peasant family, a carpenter's son. In death, Jesus identified with the lowest criminal by choosing to die condemned as a blasphemer (Mark 14:61-65) and political conspirator (John 19:12). Jesus identified Himself with the lowest level of humanity so that those on that level and higher – in their view – could experience the transforming touch of His risen life. No one is excluded or outside of the reach of Christ's gifts.

Christmas isn't a once a year event of carol singing, pretty lights, giving and receiving gifts and parties. Christmas is a daily heart matter. Those who know Jesus as Lord and Saviour recognise the significance of the rest of the day's reading. This Jesus had been raised from the bottom rank of miserable humanity to be highly exalted. He has received a Name unsurpassed in history and eternity. How then, should we respond to Him? The bowed knee illustrates the point, and the spoken word confessing Him as Lord emphasises the fact. We have the choice to do that by faith right now. One day people will declare it without choice.

Prayer: The choice you made for the likes of me is beyond my understanding, Lord Jesus. I try to plumb the depths of your love and constantly discover there is more to explore. I bow before you in wonder and lift my heart in praise to your holy Name.

My gift to Jesus today is to recognise His specific gift to me, be thankful for it and express my pleasure in worship and lifestyle.

Heavenly Bread

Day: 22

Reading: John 6:25-59

The first use of bread is in Genesis 3:19: 'By the sweat of your face you shall eat bread until you return to the ground, for out of it you were taken.' (NRSV). It also means sustenance or food. Adam's treachery introduced hard labour into the attempt to satisfy the need of body and soul. The awful reality is that such effort never succeeds in bringing complete satisfaction.

I find it intriguing the way God ties such incidental things into His plan of salvation. Where was Jesus born? Bethlehem! What does its name mean? House of bread! What a prophetically named place! The significance would lie dormant for thirty years until, by the Sea of Galilee, Jesus fed over five thousand people. After the clean up the Lord made His point. John 6:27 tells us He said, 'Do not work for food that spoils, but for food that endures to eternal life, which the Son of Man will give you.' What Adam introduced, striving for 'bread', leaves an unquenchable famine within, as Jesus intimated by the words 'do not work for food that spoils'. By contrast, the Son of Man, the promised Messiah, would 'give food that endures to eternal life'. They must have imagined all their birthdays had come at once, as their minds thought he meant literal bread. They thought it was something for which they had to work. Their cry goes up, 'what must I do?' Humankind still wants to 'sweat' to earn what the Lord desires to give freely. He wants to give each of us Himself for He is the Bread from Heaven. To name the source is to understand its nature – spiritual not earthy.

The next day the people were hungry and wanted another miracle to feed them . Jesus doesn't comply. Instead, He urges the people to understand what He offered was a relationship with Himself. At the same time He tried to explain the purpose of His mission. Confronted by the spiritual difficulties and its implications they find it too hard to stomach. When Jesus claimed, 'I am the bread of life. Whoever comes to me will never go hungry; and whoever believes in me will never be thirsty' (John 6:35), the grumbling began. How was it possible to understand John 6:48-51: 'I am the bread of life ... I am the living bread that came down from heaven.

Whoever eats this bread will live for ever. This bread is my flesh, which I will give for the life of the world.' After the cross, did any of those hearers grasp Christ's implication behind 'my flesh which I will give for the life of the world'?

If there had been any leaven (the symbol for sin) in His life Jesus would have been left in the tomb. His resurrection declared He is the unleavened Bread from heaven to meet the hunger of the heart.

In writing to the Church in Galatia, Paul speaks of wanting the disciples to realise that Christ has been, or wants to be, formed in them (Galatians 4:19). This is beautiful, glorious imagery of what God has done in a believer. What happens in a person's life when he accepts Jesus as his 'Bread of Life'? What was previously devoid of the presence of the Lord has now become Bethlehem – the House of Bread. It defines the heart in which the Lord, the Bread of Heaven, resides. He is the one who satisfies eternally.

Prayer: As I consider what you have done for me, words fail me, my Lord and my God. You transformed my being from the haunts of evil to the haven of Grace, from a slum to a temple. For this I bow in praise before you. Amen!

My gift is to give to you, beloved Lord, my body, as a worthy expression of your indwelling. I will endeavour to guard against mixing the leaven of the world with the Bread of Heaven.

No Reputation
Day: 23

Reading: Isaiah 53:1-12

Magazines abound that are dedicated to real or imagined celebrities. Beautiful, successful and rich people walk the red carpet to the cheers of fans and would-be celebrities. Fame with or without fortune is a longing of the human heart. Many of us enjoy telling stories of our brush with someone famous. We wish his or her shadow would fall on us and bring good luck.

Jesus didn't come to earth as a celebrity fawned upon by fans and paparazzi. The passage in the above reading opens our minds to the humiliation Jesus was prepared to experience for our sake. If He wasn't willing to sink to the depths of human misery how could He lift such people up to the glories of Heaven? They could quite rightly accuse Him of not tasting their life's bitterness and, therefore, not being able to understand them. He did taste the depths of human existence! In Philippians 2:5-8 Jesus is described as a servant. The word means a slave without any rights. Such a person was disposable whenever his or her usefulness dried up. For Jesus, it would lead Him to the cross because he was a threat to the Jewish authorities and therefore expendable (John 11:45-53). Consider Hebrews 2:14-18 and 4:14-16 as the writer of that letter expresses appreciation of Christ Jesus making Himself of no reputation for us. The passage speaks of how Jesus, the disposable slave, was able to free those who were in slavery to the fear of death. The outcome of Christ's humiliation and identification with humankind made Him our merciful and faithful High Priest continually in the presence of God.

Philippians 2:5-11 is considered an ancient hymn. There is something in the person and work of Jesus which creates a longing to write and sing songs about Him and His impact upon our lives. It began in the early Church and has continued unabated. Paul takes this hymn and uses it to highlight the wonder of what we call Christmas and Easter. You'll notice there isn't anything sugary sweet and human centred in this hymn. It is Christ centred and stirs the heart with adoration and wonder.

What overwhelms me sometimes is the realisation that Jesus knew what was in store for Him. The passage in Isaiah 53 sums it up. He was prepared to become an object of scorn. He whom angels praised became as one without beauty and devoid of majesty. He was despised, rejected, a man of suffering and familiar with pain. He was oppressed and afflicted and cut off from the land of the living. Jesus knew all this before leaving Glory for the manager.

Christmas wants to lead you to the One who made Himself of no reputation for your eternal benefit. The Greek word for 'no reputation' is translated in the NIV as 'made himself nothing'. This self emptying by Jesus achieved the triumph over sin and Satan as foretold. Now everyone would see that the weakness of Christ is stronger than all the forces of evil (1 Corinthians 1:22-24). Our commitment to Jesus is a testimonial of His conquest over our heart and destiny. We become a forerunner of the time when He will be exalted by the Father and every tongue will acknowledge that Jesus is Lord.

Is it any wonder Christians love to sing about their Lord? Unbelievers may scratch their heads as we sing about Christ in Christmas carols and songs of the cross but we cannot help it. The Christian has something and, more importantly, Someone to sing about.

Prayer: I rejoice in the reality of what is expressed in this ancient hymn. You, Lord, came down to where I was and loved me and called me to be where you are. I am so grateful and I will praise your Name forever.

My gift is to find a way to express what is in my heart as it rejoices in your grace and majesty. Throughout eternity I will sing your praises. What a privilege!

Jacob's Promise to Judah
Day: 24

Reading: Genesis 49:8-12

On his deathbed the patriarch Jacob wanted to bless his twelve sons. These men became the tribal heads of the nation called 'The Children of Israel'. This nation was formed by God through the genetic structures of Abraham, Isaac and Jacob. It was a deliberate work of creation by Yahweh. Isaiah 43:1: 'But now this is what the Lord says – He who created you, O Jacob, He who formed you, O Israel.' Plus verse 21: 'my people, my chosen, the people I formed for myself that they may proclaim my praise.'

In Genesis 49:1 Jacob made a prophetic announcement about each son. This would impact their descendents. His words have particular bearing on a term we read for the first time in the Bible: Jacob uses 'the last days' (KJV) and in the NIV it is 'in days to come'. This term is undefined but clarified by later prophets. Jacob outlines certain features of it, especially in regard to Judah. The old patriarch wouldn't have foreseen what we call 'Christmas' but he did 'see' the Promised One. In Genesis this One is seen as the 'Seed' (offspring) born of a woman (3:15); 'Shepherd' defining benevolent rule (49:24); and 'Rock' expressing permanency and shelter. Jacob said the tribe of Judah would provide the one who would hold the sceptre and the ruler's staff. This would be well into the future, but it happened. David became the shepherd king and we can trace his lineage to the clan of Judah. From him would come the One who would claim the eternal allegiance of all.

Jacob's vision was completed in Jesus. He measures up to all the requirements of the prophecy. The Gospels of Matthew and Luke give impressive details about the lineage of Jesus. He is of the tribe of Judah. The letters of the apostles as well as the history of the Church in Acts verified it (Acts 2:29-32. Romans 1:1-3)! The rulers of the nation at the time rejected the evidence. This was the culmination of many issues, including vested interests, pride and unbelief which hardened them against Jesus even after His resurrection. This rejection still hangs over the nation of Israel. Scripture still states someday they will acknowledge Jesus as the one with the right to be the King, Lawgiver and Redeemer. Christians, by faith, agree with Hebrews 1:8, 9: 'about the Son he (God) says, "Your throne, O God, will last for ever and ever, and righteousness will be the sceptre of your kingdom. You have loved righteousness and hated wickedness; therefore God, your God, has set you above your companions by anointing you with the oil of joy".'

Jacob classed Judah as 'a lion's cub'. This aspect of his nature would find expression in the life of Jesus in the 'last days'. We can only appreciate the significance of this by realising that the promised reign of peace can only come after the victory of righteousness over wickedness. In Revelation 5:5 Jesus is called 'the Lion of the tribe of Judah'. To Him belongs the future throne within the city of Jerusalem as Jacob foretold – 'and the obedience of the nations shall be his'. They will not bow the knee to Him willingly according to Psalm 2. They will do it, if not by faith, then by defeat.

Ezekiel looked into the future and saw such a day. It has yet to take place and there are many seemingly insurmountable hurdles to 'jump'. A great thing about God is His ability to 'jump' and fulfil His word. Even when the nation was under foreign government there was an expectation of the day when the ruler's staff would be restored. Ezekiel was conscious of this even in Babylon as a 'guest' of Nebuchadnezzar, along with thousands of his countrymen. Ezekiel prophesied the destruction of Jerusalem and the overthrow of the Davidic throne by the Babylonians. He went on, however, to state the Lord's anointed will one day return to rule. Ezekiel 21:27: 'A ruin! A ruin! I will make it a ruin! It will not be restored until he comes to whom it rightfully belongs; to him I will give it.' Read Ezekiel 37:15f. Christmas completes Jacob's promise about Judah. It reveals the promised Ruler, Jesus. Now we wait His return!

Prayer: You are to me both the Lion and the Lamb. As the Lion you rule my life because you first became the sacrificial Lamb who dealt with my offending nature. To you I bow and call you Lord.

My gift to you is the sceptre of my heart and the devotion of my obedience.

Wonderful Counsellor
Day: 25
Reading: Isaiah 9:6, 11:1-11

The four descriptions of the baby son by Isaiah astounds the mind and thrills the soul. This unnamed child is destined to reign over the whole world. This will take place. It will be contested. He will prevail. Over the next four days let us consider each name separately.

The first title is 'Wonderful Counsellor'. When you compare this with Isaiah 28:29 you get a clue to whom it refers. 'All this comes from the Lord Almighty, *wonderful in counsel* (emphasis added) and magnificent in wisdom.' It would seem strange if there wasn't a link between the persons mentioned in both verses.

To be a wise counsellor requires more than academic skill, even when combined with personal experiences. Behind it all will be a worldview that influences 'the what' and 'the why' of the counsellor. Isaiah gave us his prophetic insight into the Promised One's worldview from which He would base His advice, guidance and strategies.

'A shoot will come up from the stump of Jesse; from his roots a branch will bear fruit. The Spirit of the Lord will rest upon Him – the Spirit of wisdom and understanding, the Spirit of counsel and of power, the Spirit of knowledge and of the fear of the Lord – and He will delight in the fear of the Lord. He will not judge by what He sees with His eyes, or decide by what He hears with His ears; but with righteousness He will judge the needy, with justice He will give decisions for the poor of the earth.' (Isaiah 11:1-4) The apostle John summarises this well in referring to Jesus in John 3:34: 'For the One whom God has sent speaks the words of God, for God gives the Spirit without limit.'

In reading the Gospels it becomes evident how this worldview was lived out in the dealings Jesus had with people. Whether talking with Nicodemus about being born from above (John 3), or the Samaritan woman in Ch 4 about living water, Jesus was able to penetrate to the core of their situation. When His opponents tried to trick Him over taxes Jesus stumped them with 'Give to Caesar what is Caesar's, and to God what is God's' (Matthew 22:21).

One of the many beautiful aspects of Jesus' counselling is that He understands us fully: He had created us through Adam and Eve. He knows we are 'dust'. He understands our innermost being. He realises our history and circumstances and, wonder of wonders, still loves us! You may say, 'That's all well and good for those who knew Him in the flesh, but how can we seek His face and be counselled by Him today?'

The words Jesus said to His first disciples can be applied to everyone's situations. 'If you love me, you will obey what I command. And I will ask the Father, and He will give you another Counsellor to be with you forever – the Spirit of truth ... the Counsellor, the Holy Spirit, whom the Father will send in my name, will teach you all things and will remind you of everything I have said to you.' (John 14:15-17, 25, 26). Where do we find what Jesus said to His disciples? In the Scriptures! The apostle Paul reminded Timothy of the wisdom, authority and beauty of the Scriptures when in his second letter to him, he wrote, 'All Scripture is God-breathed and is useful for teaching, rebuking, correcting and training in righteousness so that a man (and woman) of God may be thoroughly equipped for every good work' (2 Timothy 3:16, 17).

There is a marvellous Psalm which expresses the power and grace of God's Word when a person takes it to heart. Written before the New Testament, what it upholds is the total integrity of all Scripture. In relation to being God's way to counsel us, the psalmist says, 'Your statutes are my delight; they are my counsellors.' Psalm 119:24. As such they become 'a lamp to my feet and a light to my path' (Ps. 119:105).

Christmas heralds the One Isaiah wrote about. This Jesus is the Wonderful Counsellor. His word gives us wisdom so we can know Him and how to handle life. I believe you will find, in the set of descriptive titles surrounding the child born to rule, a glorious fragrance. This son who was to come – and has – would unfold the mystery of mysteries, God Himself. In the next three days we will have opportunity to meditate upon this majestic and awesome unveiling.

Prayer: Forgive me, Lord, when I have sought your counsel and, because it was too hard, I chose my own way. The wounds on my heart and the wreckage of my plans are witnesses to my stupidity. In my sorrow and need I come again seeking your advice and Spirit through your Word. I confess my need of your strength to put into practice that which you counsel. Thank you, Lord Jesus, for your mercy and understanding!

My gift to you is to believe your word and seek to live it.

Mighty God
Day: 26

Reading: Isaiah 9:6, Zephaniah 3:14-20

We all have our heroes, especially in our growing years. They are mighty creatures of myth and magic who come in the nick of time to rescue or overturn disaster. In real life there are certain people we acknowledge as being heroes. The term 'mighty' has a connotation that suggests power and heroic deeds and is often used when speaking of the military deeds of David and his soldiers.

In the context of Christmas and the person and achievements of Jesus is this a fitting term? What should we make of Isaiah's confident assertion that the coming child is not only mighty but is also God? Is Jesus merely a godlike hero acclaimed for some military success over the enemies of truth, righteousness and the Kingdom of God?

As we noted previously, Isaiah links this coming One into a unique relationship with the revelation of God in the Old Testament. The Bible is unmistakable in its portrayal of God as One. Nor can there be any lesser gods, for that is polytheism and categorically rejected by the Bible. Psalm 96:4-5: 'For great is the Lord and most worthy of praise; he is to be feared above all gods. For all the gods of the nations are idols, but the Lord made the heavens.'

Here we come to a further insight into the wonder of God. Genesis 1:26: 'Then God said, "Let us make man in our image, in our likeness."' In Matthew there's an explanation to deepen our understanding: Jesus said to His disciples, 'Go and make disciples of all nations baptising them in the Name of the Father, the Son and of the Holy Spirit ...' (28:19). Notice – *one* Name, three personalities! One Essence defining the Godhead! (John 10:30, Colossians 2:9).

Christmas is Heaven's assault in human attire on the kingdom of darkness, rebelliousness and wickedness. The One who is to come according to Isaiah is none other than *Mighty God* (emphasis added). However, He comes not as the Lord God of Hosts but as a child. He comes not as unconquerable

God but as dependent babe and dutiful son. He would be subject to the pressures and temptation of His enemies. Why?

Hebrews 4:15: 'We do not have a high priest who is unable to empathise with our weaknesses, but we have one who has been tempted in every way, just as we are — yet he did not sin.' He faced life as we do and didn't crack under the pressure.

How then does the reference to Him as 'Mighty God' have relevance for us? It points to the finalising of the promise of Christmas. The One who has gained the spiritual victory must, at the appointed time, claim the physical and territorial victory scripture details. This is the assertion as we pray, 'Our Father who art in Heaven, hallowed be your name. Your kingdom come, on earth as it is in Heaven …' Until then we are called upon to rejoice in the victory of Christ by faith. Remember the meaning of Christmas. It was an invasion, not a rock concert!

There are glorious passages recorded for all to read concerning the Lord God's coming conflict and victory. His enemies don't want you to read the Bible because it proclaims their defeat. We need to read it to strengthen our resolve when under siege or assailed by doubt and fear. Revelation, Ezekiel, Matthew and Zechariah are four of many which are worthy of your attention.

There is a psalm which is a proclamation of the Mighty God's conquest and His arrival in His earthly capital. It is Psalm 24:7, 8.

> 'Lift up your heads, O you gates;
>
> be lifted up, you ancient doors,
>
> that the King of glory may come in.
>
> Who is the King of glory?
>
> The Lord strong and mighty,
>
> the Lord mighty in battle.'

This is the child foreseen by Isaiah. Our faith in Him is actually an enlistment into the continuing conflict begun by Christ Jesus. The day of victory is foretold when we can rest from the warfare. Isaiah 2:4: 'He (the Lord) will judge between the nations and will settle disputes for many peoples, they will beat their swords into ploughshares and their spears into pruning hooks. Nations will not take up sword against nation, nor will they train for war anymore.'

Prayer: Thank you Jesus, Mighty God, conqueror of my heart, Lord of my destiny. May I be your faithful soldier in the moral and spiritual conflicts that seek to dethrone you and defraud you of your glory!

My gift to you is to be a competent soldier of the faith in the armour you have supplied.

Everlasting Father

Day: 27

Reading: Isaiah 9:6, 1 Peter 1:3-12

Difficult! That's the best way to put it. Of the four titles for the Promised One in Isaiah 9:6 this one is the most challenging. Usually we simply read it without bothering to understand it. Our knowledge of the Godhead as Father, Son, and Holy Spirit comes between us and this title. The coming ruler isn't the Father. The title presented to us by Isaiah has everything to do with the Messiah's unique role in redemptive relationships.

The term 'father' is applied to a man in a number of different ways. Of course he can be the father of children, but a childless man can be called 'Father' because he gave 'birth' to some discovery or founded a new country. Ataturk is called the 'Father of modern Turkey', Galen is the 'Father of modern medicine' and so the list goes on.

How then, can the child of Isaiah 9:6, be called the 'Everlasting Father'? He must give birth to someone or found something new. This is true of the One we are considering. The birth which defines Him as 'Everlasting Father' is spiritual. Without Him we would remain dead in trespasses and sin, useless to God and eternally adrift from His presence (Ephesians 2:1-3). Our condition was terminal. This isn't simply about exiting from this life and becoming dust. Rather, it is a state of consciousness where the eternal God is unable to be enjoyed. It is the realm of grief and regret (Luke 16:19-31).

The Godhead decreed that new life, usually termed 'being born again', is in and through Jesus Christ as Lord and Saviour. 'Christ's love compels us, because we are convinced that one died for all, and therefore all died. And He died for all, that those who live should no longer live for themselves but for Him who died for them and was raised again ... Therefore, if anyone is in Christ he is a new creation; the old has gone, the new has come!' (2 Corinthians 5:14, 15,17).

This is why the Gospel of John emphatically and consistently presented to us the imagery of Jesus being 'Life'. Heaven requires His quality of life to be the animating source of a person's being. Only that can endure the presence of God's glory and eternity. If this life is in Jesus Christ how can you and I receive it and know its internal reality? 'To all who received Him, to those who believed in His name, He gave the right to become the children of God – children born not of natural descent, nor of human decision or of a husband's will, but born of God.' (John 1:12, 13).

How do we receive Him? By Faith! That is, taking Him at His word and believing who He is and what He has achieved on our behalf. What do we have to believe? In John 20:31: 'These (the Gospels) are written that you may believe that Jesus is the Christ (Messiah) the Son of God, and that by believing you may have life in His name.' Hand in hand with understanding and believing in Him goes this requirement: 'If you confess with your mouth, "Jesus is Lord", and believe in your heart that God raised Him from the dead, you will be saved. For it is with your heart that you believe and are justified, and it is with your mouth that you confess and are saved.' (Romans 10:9, 10).

Faith is not blind! Nor is it a 'whistling in the dark'. Faith is the result of weighing up the evidence found throughout the whole of Scripture. Then, checking it against the historical realities, you realise there could be no Church or transformed life without Jesus and His cross and resurrection. When you do that and commit your life to Jesus as Saviour and Lord, you have the assurance of the Christmas title, Everlasting Father, being true in your life. Jesus has become the means of your new birth, for His everlasting life dwells within.

When the prophet used 'everlasting' it was with definite intent. As the term 'Mighty God' highlighted, the coming One was from eternity and came into time and space with specific purposes, strategies and tactics. When Jesus dwells within we have the wonderful hope of sharing eternity with Him and seeing Him face to face. As far as I'm concerned, that is an unending Christmas celebration.

Prayer: You created me, now you have reclaimed me. I understand the implications of the title, Everlasting Father, for you have given me eternal life. I thank you, Lord.

My gift is my devotion as a child born again into your family with a desire to honour the family Name.

Prince of Peace

Day: 28

Reading: Psalm 46:1-11, Isaiah 9:6,7

Unwrapping Christmas gifts is a pleasure to do and to watch. There is something extra special about being surprised by receiving a longed for but unexpected present. On the other hand, disappointment is deep when an expected and longed for gift isn't given. Surely, if we are totally honest, at least some of us are bitterly disappointed that the peace promised at Christmas has not eventuated.

Why the disappointment? Has the Lord failed? Has He postponed the day? Have we misunderstood the message about the Prince of Peace? How do we understand what He means by peace? Isaiah viewed the coming of the Prince of Peace in the context of a battle won. Who would be the conqueror? A child, the son given! When he described the scene, the prophet seemed to have a vision of the completion of the baby's entrance into this world. For us it remains in the future. For the prophet it was an accomplished fact.

Since the Christmas event climaxed in the cross, followers of 'the child, the son given'– Jesus Christ – have waited for the final triumph. Remember, Jesus made His intentions plain in regard to the coming conflict and the basis for peace. He placed before His hearers the necessity of making a personal choice. They are either with Him or against Him. In parable and metaphor, explicit teaching and promise, hearers were left in no doubt about the conflict in the last days. Unbelief and self righteousness mixed with various threats are strategies the kingdom of darkness uses to befuddle the call to Christ.

Another approach is to hold peace conferences and promise an illusory peace as something that can be achieved soon. This can never be fulfilled for two reasons. One is due to the human heart being deceitful and desperately wicked. The other is the very nature of the god of this world. He is a murderer and hates all who belong to Jesus! There can be no peace from either of those two sources.

Peace is a gift, not in a box, bottle or conference, but in a relationship. This is true whether we desire inner personal wholeness or global unity. This longing is impossible for humanity to fulfil. Peace can only be given by the Prince of Peace. John 14:27: 'Peace I leave with you; my peace I give you. I do not give to you as the world gives.' What is the condition required to enter into this peace relationship? Romans 5:1, 2: 'Therefore, since we have been justified through faith, we have peace with God through our Lord Jesus Christ, through whom we have gained access by faith into this grace in which we now stand. And we rejoice in the hope of the glory of God.'

The Lord didn't come to earth to negotiate. He came to conquer! Peace is the result of victory on the moral, spiritual and earthly battlefield. By faith we enjoy peace in the personal spiritual and moral realm while we await the global one. Only when that final victory takes place will such passages from Isaiah and the Psalms be fulfilled. When we call Jesus Prince of Peace, we are making both a personal testimony of what He has done for us and also a prophetic affirmation. 'He makes wars cease to the ends of the earth; He breaks the bow and shatters the spear, He burns the shields with fire. Be still, and know that I am God; I will be exalted among the nations, I will be exalted in the earth.' (Psalm 46:9, 10).

Until this final victory is realised, those who claim Jesus as the promised Prince of Peace, are to live as children of peace. Hebrews 12:14: 'Make every effort to live in peace with everyone and to be holy; without holiness no one will see the Lord.'

Prayer: For far too long, Heavenly Father, I resisted Jesus, the Prince of Peace. I can remember the day He conquered my heart for then I knew pardon, peace and a sense of well being. I long for the day when He returns to claim that which is rightfully His.

My gift is wrapped up in my 'feet'. I pray that you will use my feet so wherever I walk I leave the imprint of your peace.

Mystery Men

Day: 29

Reading: Matthew 2:1-12

Who are they? Where do they come from?

Of the many intriguing and controversial issues within the pages of the Bible, the Magi come near to the top of my list. Were they real? Are they a myth? As this is a devotional, not an apologetic statement, I will not debate their existence. Instead, I will draw from the Gospel's account some features to encourage us in our walk of faith.

At Christmas time there are many nativity scenes that impress sentimental images on our minds. Unfortunately, the scenes depicted are not always Biblical. This is especially so in regard to the Magi being by the manger with the shepherds.

Luke records the ongoing Jewish requirements following a baby's birth, including circumcision on the eighth day and the purification of the mother after forty days. This means their living arrangements had changed. Most visitors for the census would have returned home. When the Magi came to visit it was to a house, not the typical cave-type scene.

They came from the East.

The mention of their coming from the East is also highly significant when you read some of the references to the East. In many passages in Genesis and Judges, the East is portrayed as moving away from the purposes of God, or as an enemy coming to attack the people of God. The mention of the Magi indicates that, even in such hostile territory, the awareness of the Promised One still had a foothold. It should always encourage us when we recall God has not left Himself or His purposes unknown within the cultures of the world. This is realised when you read of the many cultural stories relating to the account of Noah's flood.

We do not know what motivated their interest in the coming Messiah or how they understood from seeing His star that He had come. Some authorities infer that the influence of Daniel in Babylon over five hundred years earlier laid the foundation for the Magi's visit. For whatever reason, these men came. The record of them gaining an audience with King Herod implies they were men of influence. They would not have travelled alone across dangerous territory. Nor is it credible to imagine that wily Herod hadn't sent someone to follow their movements after hearing their story. This makes their night time escape out of Bethlehem more dramatic and miraculous. What the Lord God did for Hezekiah could be applied to these mystery men. 'The Lord saved Hezekiah ... from the hand of Sennacherib king of Assyria and from the hand of all others. He took care of them on every side.' (2 Chronicles 32:22).

When they entered into the child's presence they worshipped and offered gifts. Both these acts indicate the worthiness of the child and aspects of His mission. Gold is symbolic of glory, the realm of Jesus. Frankincense is symbolic of the fragrance associated with the temple sacrifices. This pointed to the offering of Christ as a fragrant offering to God on our behalf (Ephesians 5:2). Myrrh speaks about His death, which overshadowed all His earthly life. At His birth death stalked him through Herod's madness. After the synagogue service in Nazareth Jesus aroused the anger of the people. They drove Him out of town and tried to throw Him over a cliff (Luke 4). For healing on the Sabbath some wanted to destroy Him (John 5:18). Also check out John 7:1 and 8:37.

The truth about these mysterious men may never be uncovered. However, the importance of what they did is still a challenge to our devotion and faith. Those men risked life, reputation and fortune to find Jesus. They discovered the truth of 'For I know the plans I have for you, declares the Lord, plans to prosper you and not to harm you, plans to give you hope and a future. Then you will call upon me and come and pray to me, and I will listen to you. You will seek me and find me when you seek me with all your heart. I will be found by you ...' (Jeremiah 29:11-14).

Prayer: What can I offer you, Lord, from myself and my circumstances in life? In reality, you don't need anything I have, except myself. Is there something you require of me that I alone can do? If that is so, I place my life in your hands.

My gift is my heart. Take its treasures; they belong to you. Fill me with your presence so that I can confess truthfully that the treasure of my heart is Jesus, my Lord and Saviour.

He's a Star!
Day: 30

Reading: Numbers 24:15-19, Revelation 22:16

'He's a star!' is often a newspaper headline as some newcomer makes his mark in the sporting or theatre realm. When we read such a statement we do not imagine a shining object in a night sky, we understand it to refer to his bursting onto the World's stage and consciousness.

It is ironic to read in the book of Numbers how Balaam, a pagan soothsayer, was compelled to announce the future 'Star' of Israel. This 'Star' would be the one to hold the sceptre of that nation. As you read the context, it is apparent the coming Star is intent upon a campaign of conquest.

Balaam is a most fascinating figure in Scripture. Against his will he is forced by the Lord God Almighty to bless the nation of Jacob when he was paid to curse it. The tragedy of this man is mirrored across the centuries. He knew the truth, but held it in unrighteousness. Money was his sovereign. Balaam's life is aptly summed up in Romans 1:18-19: 'The wrath of God is being revealed from heaven against all godlessness and wickedness of men who suppress the truth by their wickedness, since what may be known about God is plain to them, because God has made it plain to them.'

When Balaam received the oracle he said, 'I see him, but not now; I behold him, but not near.' The One he saw had an appointment with the future. Balaam was under no illusion about certain aspects of this coming. It was to engage in warfare and to rule the nations through the nation of Israel. There is a majestic psalm applicable to the person foreseen by Balaam. Part of Psalm 45: 'You are the most excellent of men and your lips have been anointed with grace, since God has blessed you for ever. Gird your sword upon your side, O mighty one; clothe yourself with splendour and majesty. In your majesty ride forth victoriously on behalf of truth, humility and righteousness; let your right hand display awesome deeds.'

Why was Jesus given the prophetic title of a 'Star'?

The apostle Peter presents us with an explanation couched in beautiful imagery. 'We have the word of the prophets made more certain, and you will do well to pay attention to it, as to a light shining in a dark place, until the day dawns and the morning star rises in your hearts.' (2 Peter 1:19). Jesus will usher in a new era across the world when He establishes the Kingdom of God. Before that time He makes a more personal and intimate approach to us. He wants to be the 'Morning Star' of the Kingdom of God in our hearts. Unless He becomes that to me and you, we will not participate in His coming reign.

The book of Revelation from chapter six to chapter twenty unveils the dark night preceding the rising of the Morning Star. In the writings of the apostle John we come to an understanding of the forces aligned against the Messiah. There is outlined the coming conflict of Truth against Deceit, Light against Darkness and Eternal Life against Everlasting Death. In this magnificent book we are caught up in the climax of the Christmas event. The Gospel accounts outline Christ's first phase of warfare with the powers of darkness. He did this to conquer sin, Satan and death on our behalf. In the final book of the Bible we are given a look into the next phase of the Heavenly conflict. This book is saturated with the person and strategies of Jesus Christ designed to strengthen our Faith in tough times and increase our devotion at all times. There isn't any excuse for men and women not to be aware of what lies ahead. Forewarned means you are responsible for accepting the offered protection of God from the great, horrible and final conflict.

In the final chapter of Revelation when the conflict is ended we have the following words of Jesus: 'I, Jesus, have sent my angel to give you (through John) this testimony for the churches. I am the Root and the Offspring of David, and the bright and Morning Star.' The One Balaam saw as in the future is here proclaimed as ruling and reigning. His victory brought in the long awaited and desperately desired Kingdom of God. For that glory we wait!

Prayer: Even so, Lord Jesus, come!

My gift to you, Lord, is to wait, watching for your return in glory.

Giving is the Joy of Christmas
Day: 31
Reading: John 3:16-21, 1 Corinthians 1:1-9

Around Christmas, church and community service organisations have special lunches and other treats for those struggling with life. This is a joyous time for those who give and those who receive these gifts. The source spring of such action, whether recognised or not, comes from the acts and words of God Himself. The God revealed in the Scriptures is the God who gives.

Christmas is the high point of God's willingness to give. As a song puts it, 'He gave His Son, what more could He give ...' and yet, because of this unprecedented act we are also recipients of other gifts from His 'hands'. It's an interesting exercise to go through a concordance and underline the giving nature of the Eternal and Gracious God. Some try and create a divide between the God revealed in the Old Testament and the Jesus of the New. The similarities are far greater, especially when it comes to giving.

Wrapped up in the swaddling clothes of Jesus were numerous 'Christmas presents' for men and women across the world. Often we are not conscious of them because we are focused on the greatest gift of all, Jesus Himself. Paul's letter to the Ephesians opens up the eyes of the readers to the 'side' gifts we have in Christ Jesus. 'Praise be to the God and Father of our Lord Jesus Christ, who has blessed us in the heavenly realms with every spiritual blessing in Christ.' (Ephesians 1:3.) Paul then goes on to list some of those blessings.

There is the gift of adoption as God's children to those previously considered aliens. Wrapped in red is the gift that was beyond our capacity to purchase. Inside is our redemption from Sin's slave market, accompanied by the declaration of forgiveness. As if that wasn't enough, there is a personally addressed Christmas card advising the receiver of an extraordinary and eternal 'warranty' to each and every person who accepts God the Father's gift of His Son. Paul puts it this way in Ephesians 1:13, 14: 'You also were included in Christ when you heard the word of Truth, the Gospel of your salvation. Having believed, you were marked in Him with a seal, the promised Holy Spirit, who is a deposit guaranteeing our inheritance until the redemption of those who are God's possession – to the praise of His glory.'

Jesus came to make the Christmas promises real. He doesn't offer empty 'boxes' or vain promises. For Him, the Christmas event was hand to hand combat, which lasted the length of His earthly ministry. If we lose sight of this we could so easily develop the attitude that the heavenly gifts are our right rather than an act of God's grace.

When the Spirit of the Lord Jesus reigns within, there is an 'itch' which needs to be 'scratched'. For the Lord will bring us into situations and opportunities designed to unleash His nature towards others. He doesn't ask us to do this without first preparing us, consciously or unconsciously, to take up the challenge. The 'itch' is the desire to give. The 'scratching' is when we give what is required. In doing so, the quote of Jesus recorded in Acts 20:35 comes true personally: 'It is more blessed to give than to receive'.

Paul, in his letter to the Galatians, seems to sum up the personal fulfilment of Christ's coming. Galatians 2:20: 'I have been crucified with Christ and I no longer live, but Christ lives in me. The life I live in the body, I live by faith in the Son of God, who loved me and gave Himself for me.'

Prayer: I could never attain your standard, Lord. I was desperate and unworthy. Your love reached out to me and gave me yourself through your Holy Spirit. I say thank you for your giving heart.

My gift is to follow your heart by seeking opportunities to be one who gives in the name of Christ Jesus.

The Battle Cry of Christmas

The clarion call of Heaven,

Was the battle cry of Angels

Piercing the darkness

Of the night

And the soul!

Demons cowered.

Shepherds dismayed

Believers

In the Promised One!

Glory to God in the Highest

Is the marshalling call

For all who honour Him

To enlist

In the task!

Planned by Grace

Enslaved sinners

Redeemed

In the Promised One!

Peace on earth to men

And women of good will

Angels proclaim

With delight!

Heaven's

Mercy offered

To fallen world

Wrapped

In the Promised One!

The clarion call of Heaven

The Angels battle cry

Echoes across time

Shattering

Satan's hold

Over people!

Salvation now

Possible

In the Promised One!

Raymond N. Hawkins

www.ingramcontent.com/pod-product-compliance
Lightning Source LLC
Chambersburg PA
CBHW071029080526
44587CB00015B/2551